MW00817520

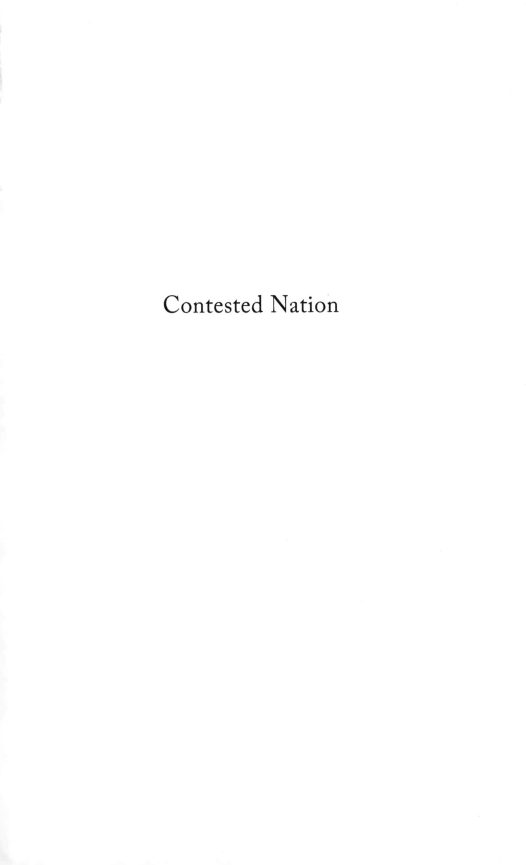

Contested Nation

Contested Nation

The Mapuche, Bandits, and State Formation in
Nineteenth-Century Chile

Pilar M. Herr

University of New Mexico Press ✑ Albuquerque

ISBN 978-0-8263-6094-6 (cloth)
ISBN 978-0-8263-6095-3 (electronic)

Library of Congress Control Number: 2019950235

Cover illustration: "Mapa de una parte de Chile que comprende el terreno
donde pasaron los famosos hechos entre españoles y araucanos" by
Tomás López de Vargas, 1777. Collection Biblioteca Nacional de Chile.
Designed by Felicia Cedillos
Composed in Adobe Caslon Pro

CONTENTS

ACKNOWLEDGMENTS

Writing this book has been a journey in itself. First, I'd like to thank my colleagues and friends at the University of Pittsburgh at Greensburg (Pitt–Greensburg), who in separate ways encouraged me. Sayre Greensfield, thanks for the many conversations; Stacey Triplette and Bill Campbell, thanks for reading portions; Eric Kimball, without you, the history program wouldn't be as strong as it is; Nancy Estrada, Anne Czerwinski, Lipika Mazumdar, and Jackie Horrall, thanks for the many conversations, laughter, tears, and your friendship. Second, I'm grateful for the many talented undergraduate students at Pitt–Greensburg I have had the pleasure to teach for the past two decades, many of whom provided suggestions over the years. A special thanks go to my exceptional undergraduate research assistants James Weir and Alex Fell.

Professional colleagues also aided me in this endeavor, and I'd like to especially thank Owen H. Jones and John Bawden for helpful encouragement in dark times; Bryan DeLay for inviting me to present at the American Historical Association conference and quietly encouraging me to write the book; David A. Nichols for reading an early draft; and Peter Guardino and Erick D. Langer, who have believed in this project since the beginning.

Thank you to the many helpful archivists of the Archivo Nacional de Chile in Santiago for their assistance in obtaining valuable primary source materials; thanks to the reviewers who provided invaluable advice and suggestions; and thank you W. Clark Whitehorn at University of New Mexico Press for your willingness to support my project.

I'd like to thank my parents and sister, as well as my extended family in Chile, for lots of hugs, words of advice, laughter, and love. Lastly, I dedicate this book to my husband, Andy, and my daughters, Sofia and Clara. Without them, this book would not exist.

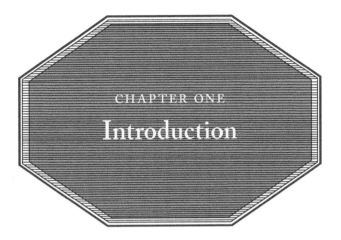

CHAPTER ONE

Introduction

ON NOVEMBER 25, 1825, THE PINCHEIRA BROTHERS AND THEIR Pehuenche allies set out to raid Parral, a town outside the city of Chillán, located near the Andes cordillera (mountain range) deep in Araucanía, Chile's southern borderlands. Federal infantry guarding the area saw them approach and successfully repelled their attack. While making their escape, the Pincheiras counterattacked, killing the captain and fifty-two soldiers, leaving only eighteen to flee. Although on this occasion the Pincheiras' men were unable to capture any loot or women, on countless other raids they were successful, netting a considerable economic profit for themselves as well as a reputation for ferocity, criminality, and cruelty. Incidents such as this one became so commonplace that "the bandits considered themselves owners of the area[s] [pillaged]" and killed anyone who opposed them.[1]

Ten years earlier, el Libertador Simón Bolívar had praised Chile, claiming,

> If any American republic is to have a long life, I am inclined to believe
> it will be Chile. There the spirit of liberty has never been extinguished;
> the vices of Europe and Asia arrived too late or not at all to corrupt
> the customs of that distant corner of the world. Its area is limited;
> and, as it is remote from other peoples, it will always remain free from
> contamination. Chile will not alter her laws, ways, and practices. She
> will preserve her uniform political and religious views. In a word, it is
> possible for Chile to be free.[2]

Chilean elites did indeed consolidate political power and create a national state independent of Spain in the early nineteenth century. In addition to establishing a strong, centralized state, Chile's new leaders sought to expand Chile's geographical boundary southward to Cape Horn. This territory included Araucanía,[3] home to multiple indigenous groups known collectively as the Mapuche, whom Chile's leaders sought to incorporate into the dominant European society. The Spanish Empire never controlled Araucanía, even though the Spanish crown spent considerable sums of money in equipping a militia on the Araucanian borderlands and sent missionaries into the territory. Araucanía was also home to bandits, who controlled a lucrative trade network and allied with various Mapuche groups to maintain their economic influence in the region. After independence, Chile's leaders first worked to eliminate the bandits, whom they considered enemies, and then spent the better part of the nineteenth century attempting to subjugate the Mapuche into mainstream Chilean society while systematically removing them from their native lands to points farther south.

This study contends that Araucanía, its Mapuche inhabitants, and bandits were central to the process of state formation in Chile because after independence in 1818, territorial expansion and acquisition beyond Araucanía became the state's primary goal. In trans-Araucanía, both Mapuches and bandits vehemently opposed state expansion but for different reasons, explored at length in this book. Mapuches fought for autonomy and independence against state encroachment upon their lands and their culture, and bandits opposed the Chilean state because it prevented the expansion of their lucrative trade in cattle and other goods. A close look at this period through the lens of Chilean–Mapuche relations aids in understanding early state formation during Chile's dual process of territorial acquisition and cultural and political conquest of Araucanía.

Additionally, the disputed behavior of these bandits and Mapuches affected and influenced the actions Chile's leaders undertook in drafting and passing the 1833 constitution, which emphasized law and order and mirrored the state's perceived need to maintain social control in its territories. Furthermore, it laid the institutional foundation for Chile's lengthy period of political stability, which lasted well into the twentieth century; allowed the newly created nation-state to embark on a lengthy and extensive geographical conquest of territories south of the boundary line at the Bío-Bío River;

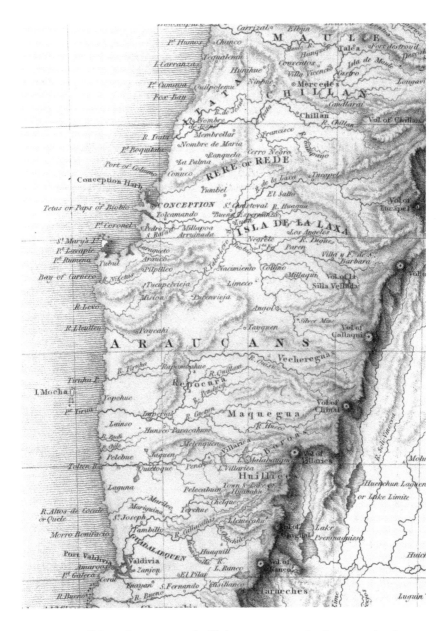

Map 1. "Mapa de una parte de Chile que comprende el terreno donde pasaron los famosos hechos entre españoles y araucanos" by Tomás López de Vargas, 1777. Collection Biblioteca Nacional de Chile.

and included legislation aimed at subsuming and incorporating indigenous peoples as well as former bandits in that territory into the newly established Chilean state. This legislation resulted in an Indian pacification[4] program that the state did not fully implement until after 1884. Nonetheless, the state simultaneously denied these peoples proper citizenship as full Chileans because of their ethnicity and position as subalterns, which led to decades of periodic violence between the Chilean military and the Mapuche in Araucanía. The presence of a frontier army in the disputed territory belied the perceived notion that Chile had achieved stability and peace. Institutional stability, therefore, took some time to emerge precisely because Araucanía, a substantial area of the country, remained a contested region until the late nineteenth century.

Scholars have tended to think of Mapuches as an exceptional ethnic group because they successfully maintained their independence from the Spanish Empire. This study argues that the ability of Mapuches to strategically utilize *parlamentos* (peace negotiations), as well as their economic dominance throughout the colonial period, provided them with not just political autonomy but actual political independence. Yet it is precisely these same mechanisms that allowed the newly formed Chilean state to dismantle Mapuche economic networks and take advantage of Mapuche internal political conflicts to subjugate them to state control. This study, then, explains why Mapuches were exceptional and expands the historiography on Indian agency by including them as an essential element of how and why state formation in Chile developed, and how Chile became known for its political and institutional stability in the nineteenth century.

Mapuche is an umbrella term for several indigenous groups of Chile's southern frontier who speak the same indigenous language. Subgroups include Pehuenches, Huilliches, Abajinos, Costinos, Boroanos, and Araucanos. The Mapungdung language, which all groups have in common, also links the different indigenous groups of central-south Chile and parts of modern-day Argentina.[5] Guillaume Boccara[6] argues that the Mapuche were in fact not Mapuches until the nineteenth century. Before this period, Mapuches went through a process that Boccara terms *ethnogenesis*, by which, as Reches, they resisted and acculturated certain aspects of the system imposed on them by the Spanish and emerged as Mapuches in the nineteenth century. His central thesis states that the Reches/Mapuches did not assimilate into the dominant Spanish–creole society but rather utilized aspects of that society to further enhance their own ethnically unique society, separate and autonomous from that of the colonial state. I follow this line of reasoning in this study, because while periods of peace and religious conversion existed during the colonial period, Mapuches never fully capitulated to the Spanish colonial government's demands, and they continued to function as independent entities within their own territories in Araucanía.

Even though the different Mapuche groups shared a common language and a large geographical area (Araucanía), they differed in their principal subsistence activities and relations to the land.[7] The Huilliches (from *huilli*, meaning "south") lived south of the Imperial River. They harvested fruits and berries found on the forest floor and in the lake region of the southern cordillera and on the island of Chiloé. The Pehuenches (from *pehuen*, or "pine," and *che*, or "people") lived along the western inclines of the cordillera and harvested the pine nuts of the *araucaria* tree.[8] All groups lived in three distinct geographical locations, or *futamapu*. There was the *lavquenmapu* (coastal region), the *telfunmapu* (the llanos region), and the *inapiremapu* (piedmont region of the Andes cordillera).[9] Each futamapu had many *ayllarewe* (a group of nine *rewe*, or loosely defined familial units) under one *ulmen*, or "grand man."[10] The general sociopolitical structure of Mapuches was decentralized, as was their economic base. For the most part, Mapuches were self-sufficient, depending on hunting and subsistence farming. They also traded across the different futamapus and among the different Mapuche communities. Each division, including Pehuenches, functioned within their individual communities and territorial futamapus, with little overlap among the different groups.[11] In times of war, however, each rewe had a boss of war (*gentoqui*) and a boss of peace (*genovoye*). These bosses made decisions for a rewe. Those who did not heed their decisions had to compensate the injured party.[12] The gentoqui and genovoye were called upon only when needed. Further, they were chosen for leadership by merit, which consisted of being exceptional warriors as well as having superior oral skills to impart wisdom in a rational manner.[13]

More recent scholarship takes a transnational approach to Mapuche territory, stressing the importance of what some scholars name the Wallmapu, defined as "all Mapuche territory" in Mapundung. Sarah Warren maintains that modern Mapuche intellectuals in both Chile and Argentina emphasize the Wallmapu as the opposite of the traditional notion of nation-state borders, in which inhabitants create their own transnational border "as a way to disregard borders, emphasize a common territory and identity, and avoid using the language of the states."[14] This transnational approach understands the Wallmapu, rather than physical territory, as the center of "Mapucheness," emphasizing the cultural production of flags, maps, a common language, and literature that express a sense of cohesiveness among the Mapuche of Chile and Argentina, and "giv[ing] indigenous peoples a sense of the power and wealth they have and what they have been deprived of. . . . By opening up a transnational vision of the world, it allows people to stop seeing like a nation-state."[15] In the nineteenth century, the Wallmapu may have existed, and Mapuche leaders interacted on both a "national and transborder level," as Warren asserts, but as this study illustrates, Mapuches (at least those on the western side of the cordillera) were also concerned with protecting their territory and maintaining their political and economic autonomy from a nation-state that considered Araucanía its southern national border.

From the sixteenth to the eighteenth century, different Mapuche groups controlled large commercial networks, trading among themselves as well as with Spanish–creole settlers on both sides of the Andes cordillera. The main commodities were cattle and horses, but other products, such as salt, wheat, corn, tobacco, and alcohol, were included:

> During times of peace there was the opportunity for the development of commerce with the indigenous towns, when both parties were interested. Three or four caravans, loaded with goods, would head to determined points deep into the Andes to trade with the Indians. They would trade wheat, corn and metal products for salt and cattle. This trade must have been very successful because for three rings of iron to use with a horse's bridle, the Indians would give two horses or one fat cow. For wine and tobacco, they paid any price, and even though there was a strict prohibition and even ex-communion on these products, alcoholic beverages, arms and gun powder were exported.[16]

Horses, which the Spanish introduced to Chile in the sixteenth century, became an important Mapuche commodity, both for the extensive and lucrative market in cattle and other goods and for resistance against the Spanish and later the Chilean state.[17] One foreign traveler in Chile in the early nineteenth century described Mapuche horses as "constituting one of the objects of early commerce, and still very much admired; they are recognized by certain exterior features, above all the wide face and large hooves, which are shapeless but very useful over lava. . . . They are very good at resisting even the Chilean race, and are as sure-footed as mules in the high mountains."[18]

Conchavadores (merchants) dominated colonial trade and acted as middlemen between Mapuches and the Spanish–creole settlers in Araucanía.[19] After independence, the economic landscape would begin to change. Fighting between creole patriots and royalists (those loyal to the Spanish crown) would disrupt commercial networks in Araucanía and elsewhere because those fighting were part of either one group or the other. Mapuches fought on both sides of the conflict. By the mid-1820s, the royalists, now defeated, would lose their economic networks to the newly expanding Chilean Republic. From 1810 to 1830, Chilean patriots fought against Spain for independence while simultaneously seeking to consolidate a strong, centralized republic.

Independence and *la guerra a muerte*

Bernardo O'Higgins, the Argentine general José de San Martín, and the army San Martín brought across the Andes were the heroes of Chilean independence. After the patriot defeat on March 19, 1818, at the Battle of Cancha Rayada, where O'Higgins was severely wounded, San Martín regrouped. On April 5, 1818, he and O'Higgins defeated the Spanish general Mariano Osorio on the plains of Maipo, just outside Santiago.[20] That battle marked Chile's official independence from Spain but not the end of the Spanish presence in Chile. After the defeat at Maipo, Osorio and the remnants of his army retreated six hundred kilometers south to Talcahuano to retake Concepción and then to head north to Santiago. O'Higgins, now the leader of liberated Chile, knew the Spanish threat still existed and appointed Ramón Freire as intendant of the province of Concepción, south of the capital. O'Higgins also named Brigadier Antonio González Balcarce as commander of the force to expel the Spanish from Concepción. Osorio did not stay long in Talcahuano. He sailed for Peru (still a Spanish stronghold) in September 1818 and left the Spanish officer Juan Francisco Sánchez in charge. Sánchez became the head of the Spanish contingent in Chile, located principally in Concepción Province.[21] His administration lasted two months. In November 1818 he abandoned Concepción for Valdivia. He subsequently sailed to Peru, where he died in August 1819.[22]

His departure, however, did not signal the end of the Spanish presence in Chile's south. Before leaving, Sánchez arranged for Vicente Benavides to assume command of the Spanish army and be the representative of Spain in Chile. Benavides shared responsibilities with Juan Manuel Pico, commander in chief of the royalists on the frontier.[23] Significantly, for the next several years Benavides and Pico, with their Mapuche and bandit allies, frustrated the Chilean state's efforts at consolidating power and control in the region.

José Bengoa describes this period from 1819 to 1824, known as *la guerra a muerte* ("the war to the death"), as a guerrilla war, where cruelty and extreme violence, in the form of rape, assaults, and robberies, became routine.[24] Anarchy reigned, and the newly formed state fought to rid itself of any remnants of the Spanish while simultaneously trying to create order in a region where it historically had very little control. Moreover, beginning in 1826, political conflicts between conservatives (*pelucones*) and liberals (*pipiolos*) resulted in a civil war that ended with a conservative victory at the decisive Battle of Lircay in April 1830.[25] For the next three years, Chilean elites constructed a new conservative regime. It became enshrined in the 1833 constitution, which theoretically brought order to the chaos in Araucanía and had a profound influence on the process of state formation in Chile.

Historiography

There is a considerable historiography on state formation, borders, and indigenous agency in North America, most especially in the borderlands regions of the southwestern United States. This literature is also rich in its coverage of the colonial period (both Spanish and English) as well as much of the nineteenth century. *Contested Nation* understands the complexity of state formation in newly independent Chile as analogous to that of these borderlands regions, with similar issues of indigenous agency and state formation. Just as in the North American Southwest, the Mapuche of Chile's Araucanía fought to maintain their independence from an encroaching state that coveted their lands for economic expansion while systemically denying inhabitants basic political rights and access to emerging economic networks and political representation. Some studies on South America in the colonial period (both Spanish and Portuguese) treat frontiers and indigenous agency vis-à-vis the Spanish or Portuguese colonial state. These include various microstudies of different indigenous groups, as well as economic and political studies illustrating the complexities of these relationships.[26] Much less has been written about these subjects in the post-independence nineteenth century, however. Recent scholars are beginning to bridge the gap in regions such as the llanos in Venezuela and Colombia, various frontiers in Brazil, the littoral region of modern-day Paraguay and Uruguay, and the pampas region of Argentina.

FRONTIER OR BORDERLAND?

Frederick Jackson Turner famously defined the frontier as "the outer edge of the wave—the meeting point between savagery and civilization."[27] Scholars in the late twentieth century argued for a more complex definition, a "contested ground" where "different polities contend for natural resources and ideological control, including the right to define categories of people and to determine their organization, population, and technology."[28] David Weber defined frontiers as "zones of interaction between two different cultures—as places where the cultures of the invader and of the invaded contend with one another and with their physical environment to produce a dynamic that is unique to time and place."[29] Richard White's *The Middle Ground* (1991) similarly opened up the historiography on borders.[30] Much of the debate on borderlands in the late 1990s centered on whether competing empires shaped the conflicts in the borderlands and how the frontier relations that resulted were contingent upon those conflicts. Some scholars argued, in opposition to this view, that by placing borderlands in the context of empire and nation-state building, borderlands communities become deterministic rather than agents of their own identity and complexity.[31] Newer scholarship on borderlands has sought to place agency in the hands of borderlands inhabitants themselves and to trace and understand the diverse and unique environments that borderlands areas exhibited. In this understanding of borderlands, these are "frontier" spaces that indigenous people control. In some cases, they use imperial powers as their pawns.[32]

Contested Nation views Araucanía in the nineteenth century as a frontier zone or borderlands region inhabited by several indigenous groups that continuously fought among themselves for territorial and political control. This was also a region where bandits exerted considerable economic and political clout amid both the indigenous groups in the region and the newly formed Chilean state. Araucanía, then, was a contested borderland over which both the new Republic of Chile, and Mapuches and bandits claimed control. To the Chilean state, Araucanía constituted a crucial portion of its national territorial boundary, while Mapuches and bandits, who inhabited the region, held very different notions of what that territory meant. As I demonstrate in this study, even after the state eliminated the bandits, conflicts in Araucanía between its Mapuche inhabitants and the Chilean state were not resolved until the last third of the nineteenth century, when Araucanía ceased to exist as a separate geographical boundary altogether and Mapuches became incorporated into the national state as second-class citizens.

BANDITS

The term banditry and the classification of who is a bandit have spawned a considerable amount of writing from scholars of Latin America. Most of these works build upon Eric Hobsbawm's classic *Bandits,* first published in 1969. For Hobsbawm, bandits were essentially "prepolitical," existing mainly in agricultural societies where the state played a minimal role and popular support for their activities was high. Banditry eventually ceased to exist once agrarian society transformed under capitalism, when the state played a much larger role and support for bandits was lost.[33] More recent work on banditry in Latin America is either critical of Hobsbawm or claims a more nuanced model of bandit behavior, arguing, among other things, that contrary to being "prepolitical," peasants were bandits struggling for individualized gain and often held important ties with elites.[34] Andy Daitsman takes Hobsbawm's theory on social banditry one step further. For Daitsman, "It is not the bandits that create the concept of social banditry, but rather, the communities where they come from."[35] Furthermore, "banditry as a peasant discourse is a legitimate form of peasant resistance. . . . As a peasant concept, then, social bandits represent the reformulation of the social order in such a way that benefits the peasant community, and not that of the elite."[36]

Richard Slatta's collection *Bandidos: The Varieties of Latin American Banditry* (1987) suggests a revisionist view of Hobsbawm, arguing that contrary to being "prepolitical," bandits were peasants struggling for individualized gain and often held important ties with elites.[37] Also, scholars found family allegiance and kinship to be important factors for banditry in societies where these relationships governed with some intensity.[38] Additionally, the revisionists introduced two other classifications of bandits: "political" and "guerrilla." What distinguished these bandits from Hobsbawm's social bandit, according to the revisionists, was their alignment to either a political ideology or a particular group.[39] For example, in William Taylor's conception of banditry, bandits roamed Jalisco and outlying areas in "gangs" called *gavillas*, robbing and pillaging.[40] A typical member of a gang was "in his late twenties or early thirties, from a poor socioeconomic background, illiterate, and likely to be classified racially as a Spaniard or an Indian."[41] Eric Vanderwood, also writing about bandits in Mexico, not only supports Taylor's "gang" typology but even cites specific examples of famous banditos such as Rojas, Berthelín, and Jesús González Ortega.[42] Charles Walker, writing about Peru right after independence, describes bandits or *montoneros* (a group of men on horseback; a bandit gang) as groups of men who fought in Peru's various civil wars during this period to gain national recognition as citizens of the state.[43]

Gilbert Joseph underlines the importance of the relationship between banditry and the law and "how banditry and other strategic peasant options reflect the dynamic larger social environment."[44] Joseph and other scholars expand the study of banditry by focusing on resistance and the bandits' relationship to law and order (the state), "how banditry and other strategic peasant options reflect the dynamic larger social environment."[45]

Juan Pablo Dabove, in his 2017 *Bandit Narratives in Latin America: From Villa to Chávez*, argues that there are two ideological dimensions to the term *banditry*: the "realists" and the "nominalists." For those who conform to the realist model, the task is to figure out a set of behaviors, motivations, and actors "that can unify and homogenize the multiple manifestations of banditry and anchor a possible definition of more or less universal validity, or

ground a number of conceptual distinctions."[46] Nominalists are more interested in the uses of the term as defined by three areas: (1) signs and symbols;
(2) documents from the time; and (3) the culture of the community. As
Dabove elegantly puts it, "The defining feature is not what the bandit does
(this is usually rather clear), but rather the conflict over the representation
(hence, the value, political or otherwise) of what the bandit does."[47]

Dabove's examination of the dynamics of the purposes of using the banditry label becomes instructive when analyzing banditry as part of the process of state formation in the early nineteenth century and, in some cases, as
a continuing discourse on the authoritarianism present to this day in several
Latin American countries. For example, Chris Frazer's *Bandit Nation: A History of Outlaws and Cultural Struggle in Mexico, 1810–1920* (2006) is a cultural
history of banditry in Mexico since independence. Rather than focusing on
whether banditry is social or otherwise, Frazer is interested in the cultural
production of banditry in Mexico. He wants to know why and how Mexicans, as well as foreigners, talk and write about bandits in Mexico and what
it means to be a Mexican (*la mexicanidad*). For Frazer, "bandit narratives
were integral to broader processes, involving Mexicans and foreigners in
forms of national and class struggle, to define and create the Mexican nation-
state."[48] Furthermore, Frazer argues that banditry has had a profound influence on elites and authoritarianism in Mexico: "Banditry, and attitudes
about it, was also central to the development of an authoritarian praxis in the
process of state formation. From 1821 onward, the elites never deviated from
a belief that lower-class Mexicans were backward and dangerous. As a result,
they saw the state as a vital instrument of social control."[49]

In early nineteenth-century Chile, the case of the Pincheira brothers
becomes instructive. These four brothers hailed from the southern city of
Chillán. They had close ties to the Pehuenches of this region, who had a
profitable trade in cattle and dominated the salt business and trade in other
products in Araucanía in what is now western Argentina on the eastern side
of the Andes. The Pincheira brothers often raided local haciendas (large,
landed estates) for cattle and captives, which they then traded with Pehuenches for salt and other commodities. The Pincheiras also served as valuable
allies in the Pehuenches' continuing conflicts with other Mapuche groups in
Araucanía. The Chilean state viewed the Pincheira brothers as bandits
because they were breaking the law and therefore subject to prosecution.

Because the Pincheiras were royalists (at least through 1824) and therefore considered crown policies superior to those of a newly formed state, they were "enemies." I believe, and argue in this study, that Chile's leaders, by criminalizing political behavior, effectively delegitimized behaviors and actions that threatened their state-building project. Furthermore, because elites believed the Pincheiras were criminals, they were therefore incapable of living in the elites' nineteenth-century conception of an orderly society and became a threat that needed to be eliminated. For Chile's leaders then, society had to exist in an atmosphere of law and order, noticeably absent in Araucanía.

The Pincheira brothers were not interested or politically motivated in the creation of a postcolonial Chilean state that threatened their political and economic relationships with their Pehuenche allies in their geographic region. Hence, the Pincheira bandits, as political actors, were very much involved in opposition to state formation in Chile, a position contrary to that of Frazer's bandits, whose culture of banditry contributed to the identity of la mexicanidad. Indeed, following Ana María Contador's description of them in her study *Los Pincheira: Un Caso de Bandidaje Social, Chile, 1817–1832* (1987), the Pincheiras may have been social bandits within a community that they worked hard to protect, but their political and economic motivations, which were diametrically opposed to those of the newly formed Chilean state, were paramount. The Pincheiras were not linked with being Chilean (*la chilenidad*). Rather, they consciously acted to prevent the formation of the Chilean state because it threatened their very existence.

Consequently, being citizens of the new Chilean Republic was problematic for bandits and Mapuches. This was particularly true for the notion of family and the role of family in a nation-state. Sarah C. Chambers argues that the notion of the family played a significant role in the formation of the nation-state in Chile, particularly in the early decades of the nineteenth century. In their work to consolidate a viable nation-state, elites resorted to the trope of family by pardoning former royalist sympathizers, restoring pensions to spouses and children left behind, and, to a certain extent, returning confiscated property when it proved advantageous to do so.[50] Yet not all royalists were the same. Who became a part of Chile's *gran familia* and who did not was a direct result of the state's goals of geographical expansion and racially inflected notions of chilenidad. The last Pincheira brother, as an ex-royalist, received state citizenship, but only after proving his loyalty to the Chilean Republic by ceasing all activities that threatened state security. Thus the new republican government pardoned royalists and brought them into the new state "family." Only then did the state grant lands and privileges that enabled Pincheira to become part of the gran familia. Citizenship was a reward for those Mapuches who were loyal to the state during the turbulent 1820s,[51] but at the cost of alienating other Mapuche groups and giving up Mapuche cultural and land ownership practices. For those Pehuenches who followed the Pincheiras, who at one point also identified as ex-royalists, not only did the state not grant citizenship, but it eventually seized their lands, forcing them to make a new home in Argentina. Citizenship itself, then, and who was a good citizen in this new republic, depended on racially constructed views that elites, politicians, and travel writers who visited Araucanía documented in various writings analyzed in this book—writings that exalted Indian bravery but rewarded white loyalty and excluded indigenous peoples from citizenship.

In addition to books and articles, I used archival materials, including military dispatches, civil correspondence, legal cases, peace treaty negotiations, and religious works. Also included were personal archives, nineteenth-century Chilean histories, and newspapers. There are seven chapters, organized both thematically and chronologically.

A detailed discussion of the legal formation of the Chilean Republic is the subject of chapter 2, with a specific focus on the constitutions of 1823, 1828, and 1833. The political problems that the new state faced had geographic, economic, political, and cultural ramifications for Araucanía. The 1833 constitution and the dramatic shift to a more conservative government in the same year brought about political stability and "peace." It also left little room for those subaltern groups not considered proper citizens of the newly formed state.

Chapter 3 analyzes the role of bandits in the formation of Chile's nation-state. It discusses banditry in Chile in the early national period, focusing specifically on the Pincheira brothers and their montonera, who fought a twelve-year guerrilla war against the Chilean state that ended with the capture of the youngest of the Pincheira brothers in 1832. The significance of this war cannot be underestimated. The Pincheira brothers' influence and relationship with the Pehuenches frustrated the Chilean elite's attempts to consolidate their hold on the region both militarily, geographically, and politically. This guerrilla war and its aftermath subsequently led to the repressive measures that became law in the 1833 constitution.

Mapuche political alliances are the subject of chapter 4. These relationships were significant in that they highlight the complexity of Mapuche politics, as illustrated by the case of Mariluán on the one hand and the Pehuenches on the other. The chapter also discusses how these Mapuche alliances played a central role in the complicated independence period and the subsequent creation of the Chilean state.

Chapter 5 explores political and economic relations between the state and the Mapuche in Araucanía. The chapter addresses the continuities and changes within parlamentos from the middle of the colonial period until the middle of the nineteenth century. Tracing the changes and continuities within these parlamentos sheds light on the uniqueness of the parlamento system in the Latin American context and illustrates the new state's aggressive policy to subjugate Araucanía and its Mapuche inhabitants under state control. Parlamentos and their changing nature also provide an explanation for the Mapuche's efforts to maintain and defend the independence they had long enjoyed under the Spanish crown.

Chapter 6 examines the newly formed nation-state's perceptions of race and ethnicity through the lens of several nineteenth-century Chilean elite intellectuals and travelers to Chile, whose political views, as reflected in their writings and debates, were central to the role of citizenship in Chilean society. These intellectuals and travelers had a profound influence on Chile's nation-state-building project and are pivotal in understanding the Chilean government's racially inflected philosophy of state formation, as well as shedding light on who exactly was qualified to become a model citizen in the new republic. Royalists, bandits, and especially Mapuches were outside the parameters of civilized society and thus could not become citizens. This chapter explores this dynamic and discusses alternative notions of citizenship, as seen through the eyes of those who were denied full citizenship in the new state.

The concluding chapter discusses the importance of Araucanía to the development of the Chilean state and places this book within the larger geographical framework of borderlands societies and state formation in Latin America. Araucanía's Mapuche inhabitants played a central role in how the

new Chilean state chose to pursue a racist expansionist policy that simultaneously exalted indigenous bravery and also relegated the Mapuche to
second-class citizenship. Other subalterns, such as the bandit Pincheira
brothers, challenged the nation-state's monopoly on force and were therefore
considered criminals and enemies, and thus unfit for citizenship in Chilean
society as perceived by the state. This book considers new questions about
these subaltern groups within a borderlands framework, thereby expanding
the scope of research on borderlands and state formation in the Southern
Cone during this time period.

CHAPTER TWO

The Legal Formation
of the Chilean State

CHILE'S LEADERS BELIEVED THAT CHILE AS A NATION ENCOMPASSED all the territory from La Serena in the north to Cape Horn, the extreme southern tip of the continent, including Araucanía, Mapuche territory. Since colonial times, the Mapuche had fought to maintain their autonomy from the Spanish, and this did not change with Chile's independence from Spain in 1818. Araucanía was also the home of the Pincheira brothers, who allied with Pehuenches and from 1819 to 1832 fought a guerrilla war against the newly formed state. Chile's leaders considered the alliance between the Pincheiras and the Pehuenches a formidable threat to their efforts to establish a stable and orderly society and spent more than a decade attempting to eradicate them, with no success.

This chapter explores Chilean state formation between 1819 and 1833 from the perspective of the state. During the decade of the 1820s, the young republic endured three constitutions and numerous governments that did little to strengthen the nation-state. Additionally, the state's failure to eliminate the Pincheiras and control the Mapuche stemmed from its political disorganization and infighting at the national level. On numerous occasions throughout the decade, Chile's leaders sought to establish order and stability through the creation of various constitutions that did little to establish either. Moreover, many of the military decisions made in Araucanía during this period were linked to political events taking place in the capital, effectively making the newly established state weak and ineffective. It was not until the pelucones (conservatives) won a civil war against the pipiolos (liberals) in 1829–1830 that the political squabbling came to an end. After their military victory, the pelucones successfully consolidated and centralized power at the national level, making the pursuit of stability and order a cornerstone of their administration. The arrest of the last Pincheira brother and the scattering of his Pehuenche allies into the cordillera in 1832 enabled Chile's leaders to further consolidate state control of Araucanía. Passage of the 1833 constitution a year later formalized the new government's administration. This authoritarian constitution emphasized law and order and mirrored the state's drive to maintain social stability in its territories.

The 1820s: Political Disasters

The 1820s were a difficult period politically for Chile. Creole elites in Santiago, wanting to end the chaotic independence wars of the 1810s, sought to stabilize the young nation through a series of failed political experiments. Constitutions swung between centralist authoritarianism and extreme federalism. In 1817 Bernardo O'Higgins, the hero of the independence wars against the Spanish crown, became Chile's first leader. Although he considered himself a liberal in the late eighteenth-century European tradition, he was not very attached to liberalism's belief in rule by the people and its adherence to civil liberties and rights.[1] Instead, O'Higgins believed Chile needed a good dose of measured authoritarianism for proper state development. In 1818 he established Chile's first constitution. The charter had a strong executive branch that gave the supreme director almost unlimited power. For example, the supreme director chose members of the senate as well as members of the three ministries.[2] The supreme director also was the head of the armed forces and the militia, and had the mandate to "exercise Executive Power throughout his territory" (title IV, article 1).[3] Some restrictions to executive authority did apply. The supreme director "could not intervene in any judicial, civil or criminal manner before the courts" (title IV, chapter II, article 1).[4] As a centralist and authoritarian document, the 1818 constitution also restricted civil liberties. It justified search and seizure "in cases the Senate deemed urgent" (title I, chapter I, article 5).[5] Freedom of the press was guaranteed if "one does not offend the particular rights of the individuals in society, public peace and the Constitution of the State, the conservation of the Christian religion, pure and sacred morals" (title I, chapter I, article 11).[6] None of these provisions, however, helped O'Higgins build strong institutions to enforce his vision of a stable society. Additionally, his association with Argentine José San Martín's Lautaro Lodge, a highly secret society "dedicated to independence for the Spanish American colonies [that] swore its members to secrecy on pain of death and . . . sought to control government policy,"[7] raised elites' suspicions of his goals and made them more reluctant to proceed with his policies.

To salvage his administration, O'Higgins created a new constitution in 1822. This charter also called for a powerful executive, but in some ways it was more restrictive than the 1818 constitution.[8] Unfortunately, the new constitution came at the heels of already mounting political problems. In 1819, O'Higgins had provided amnesty to ex-royalists who surrendered to the state and had returned confiscated property to them:

BANDO—The Supreme Director of the State [O'Higgins] with the Consent of its Excellency, the Senate: At the moment that the enemy has surrendered from our territory, one of my principle attentions was the manifestation of the inhabitants of Concepción concerning the amnesty decree of the 8th of February last, in which the liberal system extended its forgiveness in order to evade the ruins of honor, property, and the lives of its subjects, giving them a pardon, and to completely forget their past actions, so that they may once again participate in society and return to their previous activities. So that the rest of the dissidents of the State may participate in this act of good faith and that they understand that the government prefers to win them over through the medium of kindness and sweetness proper to the liberal system, it declares them included under the amnesty law of the 8th of February.[9]

Santiago's elite were not pleased. O'Higgins's finance minister's involvement with speculation in the state monopoly on tobacco and other products (the *estanco*) further angered the elite class, who suspected corruption within the government. Another sticking point was a loan O'Higgins secured from England to finance his administration, which Santiago elites did not approve. There were also rumors that O'Higgins was planning to replace General

Ramón Freire, who at the time was the popular army commander at Concepción. Lastly, O'Higgins's suggestion that the senate temporarily cease its sessions and transfer legislative powers to him as supreme director[10] was too much for the political elite, who, with General Freire, rebelled, taking the cities of Coquimbo and La Serena and most of Santiago. In the end, O'Higgins could not stand the pressure. On January 28, 1823, he resigned as supreme director and left for exile to Peru, never to return to the country he helped to liberate from the Spanish.[11]

A series of other political experiments followed O'Higgins's departure, beginning with General Ramón Freire, who came to power in January 1823, and Mariano Egaña's writing of the 1823 constitution, which attempted to institutionalize order in the section entitled "National Morality" (title XXII).[12] In article 249, for example, "the legislation of the State, there will be a moral code that details the obligations of a citizen throughout his life, forming habits, exercises, obligations, education, rituals and pleasures that will transform the laws of custom and civic and moral virtues."[13] Because of its inconsistencies and contradictions, however (see titles II and XX), Chile's ruling elite ultimately failed to carry out the tenets of the 1823 constitution and General Freire resigned his post as president, telling the senate that he was unable to abide by the 1823 charter.[14] For the next three years (1823–1826), Chile's leaders experimented with several forms of government, none with much success.

In July 1826 Chile adopted a federal form of government without a new national charter. Chile's leaders divided the country into eight provinces, each with its own assembly, constitution, and considerable autonomy. Additionally, local governments exercised a broad range of authority. Nonetheless, the new nation was weak in its institutional makeup, lacking administrative and political institutions at the provincial and national level, whereby political reality did not correspond well with federalist ideology. Instead, federalism managed to deepen regional conflicts, deterring the effectiveness of the national government.[15] Santiago and Concepción ruled themselves as separate entities, often in conflict with each other.

That same year, the state rescinded the state estanco contract on tobacco and other goods that a previous administration had given to the Portales and Cea Company, run by Diego Portales and his friend José Manuel Cea. One of the guarantees of the original estanco contract, established in 1823, enabled the Portales and Cea Company to suppress contraband trade. The government at the time agreed to aid the company's efforts by providing a guard consisting of six soldiers for the protection of the stock of monopoly goods within the estanco.[16] In return for these concessions, the Portales and Cea Company was required to pay a yearly lump sum of 335,000 pesos to London for interest on the loan O'Higgins's administration had acquired. The original contract was to last ten years.

The immense power the state bestowed on the Portales and Cea Company in 1823, including the right to pursue and prosecute contraband trade, gave the company's owners political power to expand their influence beyond that of the monopoly. The estanco effectively became a "State within a State."[17] Portales and Cea were "the most feared and most important because of their influence, relationships and combined plan."[18] Hence, when the state yanked their exclusive rights to the estanco in 1826, Portales concentrated his efforts at persuading those within the existing administration who had in some way benefitted from the estanco, which easily included most of Santiago's elite. There is some speculation that Portales's actions in the late 1820s and early 1830s were to revenge the estanco fiasco, as the Portales and Cea Company came close to bankruptcy after losing the estanco contract and Portales himself was in severe financial straits throughout the early 1830s.[19] More likely, Portales believed that only a strong, centralized state could establish political and financial order, much along the lines of a successful monopoly business. Whatever the case may be, Portales became a central figure in Chilean politics toward the end of the 1820s, a subject discussed later in this chapter.

Francisco Antonio Pinto, a pipiolo, became president of the country in 1827 and adopted a liberal constitution in 1828. One of the principles of the pipiolo faction was the pursuit of individual freedoms, which allowed it to change the voting rights of citizens in the 1828 constitution. In the 1823 charter, to be a citizen with voting rights, one had to be a native or naturalized citizen, be twenty-one years old or married, be male, and meet at least one of the following requirements:

1. Own property worth 200 pesos.
2. Own a business worth 500 pesos.
3. Have a profession.

4. Have taught or brought to the country an invention, business, science or art, the worth of which is approved by the Government.
5. Have completed his civic duty.
6. All should be Roman Catholics unless accepted by the Legislature; all should be educated in the Constitution of the State; all should have been registered in the national book register, and in possession of his identification card, at least one month before the elections; all must know how to read and write (title II, article 11).[20]

These requirements limited suffrage to the elite and merchant classes, because few rural or even urban workers met them. By severely limiting suffrage rights, the 1823 charter ensured that political power stayed within the elite. Interestingly, as landowners, Mapuches were citizens under the laws of the 1823 charter, yet the state refused to acknowledge those rights.

In contrast, the 1828 charter simplified the requirements for citizenship. The basic age and marital status requirements remained the same. However, evidence of employment or being a member of a militia also qualified. Even more significant, the literacy requirement was dropped (chapter II, article 7:1).[21] In effect, the change in voting rights for citizens in the 1828 constitution enlarged the suffrage pool, since now poor rural workers and the urban poor had the same voting rights as elite citizens. In his book *Society of Equality*, James Wood studies artisans who also served as national guardsmen, which complicated the issue of loyalty to the new republic and its corrupt practices.[22] Wood discusses at length the debate about political citizenship in the newspapers of the time. On one side were those who believed that citizenship had to be earned through service. On the other side were those who had a different notion of political service, one that had to do with moral character and cultural practices. Mapuches, who remained landowners, also qualified as citizens under the 1828 charter, but the state continued to deny them those rights.

Spanish law required that all estates be equally divided among heirs, unless the estate was a *mayorazgo* (entailed estate). Mayorazgos allowed the landed elite to hand down an estate to only one heir rather than having it equally divided among several heirs, diluting their economic and political influence. The 1828 constitution's abolishment of mayorazgos, along with expanded suffrage, effectively limited the elites' political and economic power within the ruling class.

Continued political and economic conflicts degenerated into civil war in 1829. For the next year, pelucón troops under the command of Joaquín Prieto fought continuously against ex-president Ramón Freire's pipiolo forces, eventually winning the war on April 7, 1830, at Lircay. The Battle of Lircay was a watershed in Chile's political development, ushering in a new period of conservative rule that lasted for the next several decades and made a significant impact on Chilean society. The civil war's origins derived from an electoral dispute. In the fall of 1829, elections for president and vice president took place under the 1828 constitution. Under the new rules of the 1828 charter, members of militias were now considered citizens and given the right to vote. The 1828 charter also gave the right to vote to many people who had not had it under previous constitutions, giving the pipiolos the edge over the pelucones, the opposition. Ironically, however, to keep their hold on power, the pipiolos committed fraud in the fall 1829 election for president and vice president: A pipiolo sneaked into the voting area of a parish in Santiago and hid under the voting table for two hours. He proceeded to stuff three hundred pipiolo votes into the box from underneath the table. Wood outlines how Pinto's inner circle enlisted guardsmen commanders to collect guardsmen's ballots or force them to vote for Pinto.[23]

The opposition, who believed they had won by two hundred votes, found themselves at a loss to explain why they had lost by one hundred.[24] The final count had Pinto as president and Ruiz Tagle as vice president—both pipiolos. Pinto, however, decided not to be president and ceded his post to Francisco Ramón Vicuña. Congress did not accept his resignation, asserting that he had received the most votes. Congress also declared Joaquín Vicuña, who was fourth in number of votes cast, to be vice president.[25] Pinto resigned anyway, and the ensuing disagreement over the supposed illegality of the elections, a blatant violation of the newly drafted constitution, escalated into war. The outcome was a complete state of confusion, evidenced by massive disruptions in the streets of large urban centers, where rural workers and tradesmen protested the already disintegrated government.[26] In Santiago, these protests included artisans/guardsmen who "over and over, . . . expressed their contempt for a political system in which they were granted the legal right of active citizenship, only to have that right violated in practice."[27]

To win the war, pelucones and pipiolos enlisted provincial troops, local peasants, and bandits[28] to their cause.[29] Since chaos prevailed in the cities and the central government was unable to impose order, recruitment to one side or the other proved relatively easy. The pelucones' victory at the Battle of Lircay enabled the victors to use repressive tactics to restore order to the republic. The new conservative administration decreed a series of laws, beginning with the establishment of the Guardia Cívica (National Guard) of Santiago, headquartered in La Moneda Palace. Diego Portales, minister of war in the new government, was the brainchild behind the National Guard, which under his guidance became "a formal institution because of the organization and discipline that the various corps of armed citizens received."[30] Portales himself commanded one of these corps and dedicated himself to its discipline with unmatched fervor. By June 1831, the National Guard had more than 25,000 troops—uniformed, drilled, and newly equipped—who competed directly with the army and, in fact, greatly outnumbered it during the next several decades.[31] James Wood argues that part of the reason for the creation of the National Guard had to do with budget cuts, problems with inconsistent pay to the regular army, and lack of supplies. Furthermore, the National Guard was there to prevent attacks from within the country rather than from without.[32] "The trend toward the diminution of the army and expansion of the National Guard was thus a strategic decision by the governments of the 1820s to deal with the political and economic dislocations associated with the end of the war for independence."[33]

In March 1832, General Manuel Bulnes, another hero of the independence wars, captured the last Pincheira brother and his band of followers in the mountains east of Chillán, deep in Araucanía. The newspaper *El Araucano* stated that "with the capture of José Antonio Pincheira the peace and tranquility of the Republic is now assured."[34] Pincheira's capture paved the way for Chile's leaders to initiate a new program of development for Chile, "to set the citizens on the straight path of order and virtue."[35] Nonetheless, this victory only came about after a decade-long guerrilla war in the south that severely weakened the state formation process. Thus an examination of the events in Araucanía provides a better understanding of the difficulties the state encountered in its attempts to eradicate the Pincheira brothers and their allies, and also illustrates the state's utter failure in maintaining authority in this region.

The Chilean Countryside (1820–1833)

The Chilean agricultural center was in the central valley. *Latifundias* (large landed estates), worked by tenant laborers called *inquilinos*, dominated this area and were the economic heart of the nation. The partition of the country into provinces in 1828 placed already existing latifundias under the control of provincial governments. The most important agricultural goods for export during this period were cattle products and wines. Grains such as flour, barley, and wheat also were exported but did not gain prominence until after 1850, when Chile competed with Australia for the world market in wheat.[36] Because of the system of land distribution, many export-producing latifundias were concentrated in the same provinces. Consequently, some provinces were wealthier than others and were better equipped to handle labor shortages, migrations, and peasant unrest. For example, the provinces of Colchagua and Aconcagua were export regions. In Colchagua, the cities were administrative centers where trade in foreign goods took place.[37] On the latifundia, located on the fringes of these administrative centers, the "rich like the poor ha[d] been able to surround themselves with the objects necessary for the life of a civilized man."[38] The main exports were *charqui* (preserved meat), grease, and hides. Aconcagua was a relatively large province, divided into two areas in the south and two in the north. Situated close to the Andes cordillera, Aconcagua had the advantage of trade with Argentina. While Colchagua depended on raising cattle, Aconcagua's export crops tended to be more varied, including *aguardiente* (native drink), wine, and fruit.[39] Aconcagua also had gold and copper mines.

The size of the militias in the provinces was proportional to the geographic sizes of the provinces. Their relative sizes may also provide an indication of how much unrest was present in each province in any given period. In Colchagua, the militia was composed of 1,235 infantrymen and 877 cavalry,[40] signifying a relatively small geographical area to protect and possibly less peasant unrest when compared to the province of Aconcagua, whose militia had 3,101 cavalry and 1,524 infantry.[41] The size of the militias, however, was not an indicator of how efficient they were in protecting the provinces' resources or in eliminating criminal activity.

Labor on the latifundia was based on a system of *inquilinaje*. Within the inquilinaje system, several levels of workers existed. The inquilinos formed the highest level. Although they did not own land, they rented small plots on the outskirts of latifundias. Within the inquilinaje system, the *mayordomo* (manager) and *capataces* (foremen) usually held the most coveted positions on a latifundia, primarily because of their authority over others and their relative autonomy. The next level down consisted of *peones*, wage earners who did not own land. Within this level were several types of peones, including women and cattle hands. The lowest level consisted of seasonal migrants.[42] Considered a "floating population," seasonal migrants were the most troublesome to the landowners because they squatted wherever jobs were available. Problems with workers on the latifundias during this period stemmed from a lack of available jobs rather than not enough land. Nonetheless, many migrants resorted to theft rather than work for the little remuneration offered. Many also remained landless, since the large latifundias required little labor.[43] All the above categories of peasants constituted *el bajo pueblo*.[44]

Hacendados, merchants, priests, government officials, and the military ruled the bajo pueblo. They often carried out their policies with an excessive amount of violence at the physical as well as the institutional level. For the peasants, this violence meant jail time, land takeovers, shootings, and hangings. To escape repression, many sought refuge in the mountains. Some resorted to banditry and other types of behaviors.[45] The Pincheiras' montonera consistently recruited from el bajo pueblo.

Because of intense economic and political competition among themselves as well as with merchants and the military, many *hacendados* formed local militias with their inquilinos. They used these militias against any opposition, whether from the central government or others.[46] Unfortunately, the bajo pueblo usually suffered the consequences of an hacendado's disillusionment. For example, in 1829, hacendado don Francisco Porras of San Fernando initiated a series of robberies, rapes of peasant women, and the jailing of supposed opposition members. In the same year, "don Félix Novoa of Rere organized 'a small force' with which he would intercept 'public communications.'"[47]

The military practiced the same form of authoritarianism over the bajo pueblo or peasantry as the hacendados, or *hombres de poder* (men of power). During times of war, the military drafted peasants to fight the enemy. The peasants' commitment to the military, however, did not end once the wars abated. The military forced these men to continue as soldiers or to back commanders in their political maneuvers.[48] Sometimes a peasant's service to the military conflicted with his loyalty to an hacendado, causing friction between the hacendado and the military and often ending in bloody conflicts, such as the incident with don Francisco Porras.

The patron–client relationship that existed between the military, most hacendados, and peasants was one of uneven power, in which the peasants were subordinate. Although the relationship was by no means equal, it did provide a window where resistance to established norms took place. Nevertheless, any act of resistance on behalf of the peasantry induced an act of repression from the military and hacendados alike. Resistance altered the dynamics of power in the relationship between the two groups, because each act of peasant resistance required an even greater degree of military and hacendado repression. Consequently, the military and hacendados lost legitimacy in the eyes of the peasantry, and the peasants were transformed into common criminals in the eyes of the military and hacendados, who in effect were representatives of the state.

Events in Araucanía

In the southern provinces, which included Araucanía, the same latifundia system was dispersed among Mapuche communities. In the 1820s the continued royalist threat in the southern provinces prompted the Chilean state to mount campaigns against them, with mixed results. Spanish general Manuel Pico's early successes further heightened the state's fears of losing the south to the royalists, especially since his army included Mapuches who had refused to ally with the Chilean state. In addition, the Pincheira brothers offered support to Pico and his followers. For example, the Battle of Pangal, on September 23, 1820, illustrates Pico's fierceness and the state army's utter disorganization. Pico and his Mapuche allies cornered two lieutenant colonels, Carlos María O'Carrol and Benjamín Viel, in a flat area, named Pangal after a plant (*pangue*) that grows in abundance in the area.[49] Outnumbered,

O'Carrol and Viel fought valiantly, but to no avail. O'Carrol lost his life, while Viel managed to escape with only eight grenadiers.[50]

The battle at Pangal also exemplifies the state's lack of coordination in Araucanía. O'Carrol and Viel argued about military strategy the night before the ill-fated battle. Viel wanted to join the regiment of Andrés Alcázar, commander general of the frontier, farther south in Los Angeles, while O'Carrol preferred to go after Pico, who was camped nearby at La Laja. O'Carrol won the argument and proceeded to ready the force for an impending attack on Pico, resulting in his death and the virtual slaughter of the federal force.[51] "Such was the battle or better said, the slaughter of Pangal, which Pico joyfully related to the Viceroy of Peru of having won in four minutes. And that was the truth, because what resulted from that fateful day was not combat but carnage."[52]

Pico's early victories were largely possible because of disagreements between government commanders that culminated in a lack of coordination among the various forces fighting in the south. Compounding this problem was the frontier area's continued royalist support after the official independence wars ended in 1818. Hacendados, creoles, and Mapuches comprised many of the ranks of Pico's and other royalists' forces.

For example, on January 28, 1824, the commander of Ultra Bío-Bío, Luis Salazar, related the following to Pedro Barnachea, commander of arms of Concepción, "Thus I request of you, Sir, that you come to my rescue with 25 to 30 dragoniers. With these I will have the number needed to make them [the enemy] respect the state's liberal system and please send me 30 mares and 4 cows, at least, in order to continue my march, and that my mount is in very bad shape and unable to walk two days in a row."[53]

On another occasion, Commander Barnachea wrote to the intendant of Concepción, Juan de Dios Rivera, demanding horses to aid his cavalry, which was exhausted from an excursion in the ultra-cordillera: "I have already asked for the number of horses . . . thus, I guess that this cavalry is such only in name. Of those that marched in the expedition and did not get lost many are exhausted from the ultra-cordillera, and many have arrived in a lamentable state. If I don't receive these horses, it will be impossible for me to complete your orders having to do with the movements of this cavalry."[54]

Besides disorganization, the state also suffered from troop desertion, a direct result of the lack of supplies, especially food and horses. For example, six months after Barnachea's previous letter, he wrote the following to Rivera: "I add this list of deserters, assuring you that unless you, Sir, take measures against these trouble makers, we will be left, in short, without troops, according to the career they have chosen to take. It has reached scandalous proportions since between six and eight desert daily, in particular those of the Third Squadron. Here there is no motive for them to desert. Their service is less than in other areas and punishment is not with clubs. I thus do not know what to attribute to this desertion."[55]

The state's lack of knowledge of geography, the lack of supplies—especially horses—and the desertion of troops proved to be advantageous for Pico and his followers. Little is known of Pico's early life other than that he was born in Santander, Spain, and came to Chile in his youth. After the Battle of Chacabuco (1817), he hid in Talcahuano with another Spaniard. In Talcahuano he met Vicente Benavides, perhaps Chile's most celebrated enemy and at that time lieutenant of the battalion in Concepción. They joined forces and actively sought royalist support to attempt to regain Chile for the Spanish crown. For a while it looked as if their efforts might bear fruit, especially since Spaniards had a great deal of support in traditional southern cities such as Chillán, where there was a strong royalist influence. Pico and Benavides took advantage of the state's disorganization during the early 1820s to further strengthen the royalists' resolve in Araucanía.

Born in Quirihue in 1787, Benavides was the son of Toribio Benavides, the *alcalde* (mayor) of that district. Under contract with a tobacco shop in Quirihue that required him to travel to Concepción and Santiago, he left Quirihue in 1810. In 1811 he joined creole Juan José Carrera's corps of grenadiers in Santiago as a simple soldier. By 1813 he was enlisted as a sergeant in José Miguel Carrera's cavalry in Concepción. He defected to the royalists on March 19, 1814, at the Battle of Membrillar, where he was taken prisoner and escaped in the middle of a chaotic fire that broke out in the forest nearby. He later served in several more battalions and was promoted to lieutenant after the Battle of Curapalihue, on May 5, 1817, for his services as supplier. This position enabled him to make frequent trips into Araucanía, where he forged a relationship with Manuel Pico and his Mapuche allies. He subsequently was taken prisoner in Maipo and condemned to death, but General Bernardo O'Higgins suspended his sentence. Once again free, he traveled south to Concepción to gather a force to combat the state. It was with this force, which included

Mapuches, that Benavides attacked Santa Juana on February 21, 1819. The attack marked the beginning of his leadership as a royalist.[56] In a letter to a friend in December 1819, Benavides described his goals:

> Such is the picture and the lamentable scheme represented by this beautiful kingdom, sacrificed by the vile capriciousness of some of its leaders that only find glory in the annihilation of their fellow men . . . without the preponderance that independence would supposedly have on this continent, that I see briefly and which will disappear, and won't be capable of containing the solid and consistent force supported by the heroic Nations of Europe that are already in these countries, whose innocent blood that I have already seen spilled is what moves my heart, to remedy however possible the unjust luck of my fellow countrymen and friends.[57]

Benavides's successes lasted three years, and when his location was discovered, he was arrested. The state summarily tried and hanged him for treason and other unspeakable crimes.[58]

Benavides's execution severely weakened the royalist army in Araucanía. The end came with Juan Manuel Pico's death two years later. Pico had taken over Benavides's position upon his death and continued to fight battles for the Spanish crown until Lieutenant Lorenzo Coronado killed him in October 1824. Pedro Barnachea described Pico's death in a military dispatch to his superior, Juan de Dios Rivera:

> The criminal . . . this is the luck that has bypassed the assassin Juan Manuel Pico and that I have the satisfaction of announcing, Sir, remitting to you the head of this monster so that the villages may be able to see for themselves. His persistence and rebellion will not be able to be executed with the honorable arms of the patria. The knife was prepared to punish his insolence. . . . The efforts of the brave Captain Salazar and the many attempts that have been made in an effort at apprehending this villain, have delivered his head as a reward. He has died at the hands of Don Lorenzo Coronado, who at the head of a company of thirty volunteers marched to apprehend him at his lodging, and at twelve midnight on the night of the 29th of the present month Coronado

attacked Pico in his house just as he was about to fall asleep. He had just returned from a meeting with some Indians to plan an attack on la Laja. Our men were surrounded by several Indians who at Pico's cries attempted to save him, but were not able. Coronado left the house with Pico's head, and with the loss of one soldier, mounted Pico's horse and left.[59]

Pico's death marked the end of the official royalist cause in Araucanía. However, others, such as the Pincheira brothers and their Pehuenche allies, who claimed to be royalists and who had allied with Pico and Benavides before him, continued the conflict in Araucanía for several more years, preventing the state from bringing political order and stability to the country.[60]

Through its use of propaganda and parlamentos, the state gained Mapuche allies against the Pincheiras, crucially important because only they were familiar with the difficult terrain the Pincheiras called home. Once the different Mapuche groups agreed to cooperate, the state launched several military campaigns to capture and destroy the Pincheira brothers' montonera. Unfortunately, these military campaigns suffered from many of the same pitfalls that befell the previous military campaigns the state had deployed against Manuel Pico and Vicente Benavides before him, including a lack of supplies, disorganization, and the desertion of troops. General Beauchef's expedition in the summer and fall of 1826–1827 illustrates the government's ineptitude in deterring a force that threatened the state's fragile stability.

General Beauchef's Expedition, 1826–1827

General Jorge Beauchef's expedition in pursuit of the Pincheiras was a three-pronged campaign, with Beauchef leading one garrison of troops, Coronel Manuel Bulnes the second, and Lieutenant Colonel Antonio Carrera the third. General Beauchef departed from Talca on December 30, 1826. Bulnes and Carrera were to meet him at the Nequén River, deep in the southern cordillera. Pehuenches from the *reducciones* (indigenous communities) in Trapatrapa in the south, under the leadership of Cacique Levimanque and his nephew Cacique Juan José, accompanied Beauchef as guides and warriors.[61] These Pehuenches were enemies of those who followed the Pincheira brothers.

In his memoirs, Beauchef relates how he first had to convince Levimanque and his nephew that attacking Pincheira was the only way to end their oppression: "I told them through an interpreter . . . that the first thing they had to think about was an attack against Pincheira whose camp was only a day and a half's journey away and that before they talked it over among themselves I encouraged them to do so, now that they had reunited voluntarily to fight against this bandit who oppressed them."[62] To convince Levimanque to join him, Beauchef offered him aguardiente and gifts and also sent a letter to Pincheira, asking him to "end this life of banditry that is destroying his own country, promising him his life and the life of all his men if he surrenders."[63] Pincheira responded, "If you want to spend the winter in the cordillera go ahead . . . if you look for me I will attack and I will not surrender."[64] Levimanque grudgingly accepted Beauchef's offer: "For a long time, they refused to comply with my offer but I held my position. They knew I had brought them aguardiente and gifts for their women. In the end, excited from their appetite and lust they conceded to my offer. It was exactly what I wanted, because I did not trust them. They did not like to compromise themselves very much against Pincheira, whom they respected for his bravery."[65]

His reluctance reveals Pincheira's powerful influence among the Pehuenches. Levimanque knew that betraying Pincheira could mean hostilities against his territory in the future. His indecisiveness also created problems for Beauchef: "I continued my march south under the direction of the Indians of Trapatrapa . . . marching at an exhausting pace with no end in sight because only they were familiar with the routes."[66]

Once Levimanque agreed to ally with him, Beauchef wrote letters to his superiors in Concepción, which were subsequently published in local newspapers, boasting of certain victory for the state: "At last the campaign in the south has ended: Eternal glory to the savages who have spared nothing to provide peace to the nation! It is hoped that they will be imitated! Eternal glory to this dignified army . . . to the valiant commanders."[67] Official government discourse, in effect, portrayed Pincheira and his Pehuenche allies as the true savages, achieving the state's purpose of outlawing those it deemed a threat to the country's stability.

The reality, however, was quite the opposite. By July 1827, Beauchef had managed only to disperse the Pincheira–Pehuenche montonera, killing a few men and capturing some merchandise the bandits left behind in their escape.[68] The loss of these goods only stopped Pincheira temporarily. Most of the men escaped unharmed to the cordillera, where they regrouped for another attack later. On the other hand, Beauchef and his commanders experienced some hard times, including hostile weather, difficult terrain, and the desertion of troops.[69] Notwithstanding the Trapatrapa Pehuenches' initial reluctance to follow Beauchef, in the end they capitulated and supported him against Pincheira. Their delay, however, gave the Pincheira–Pehuenche montonera valuable time to assess their situation and escape. Thus, despite three able commanders, five hundred men, and several hundred Mapuches who pursued Pincheira's montonera throughout the summer and fall of 1826–1827, Beauchef failed to capture them.

Beauchef's expedition was a failure for three important reasons. First, the state's coordinated attack against Pincheira required the cooperation of the Trapatrapa Pehuenches. Without them, the plan was certain to fail. The Chileans' ignorance of the terrain and Beauchef's mistrust of the Trapatrapa Pehuenches made the indigenous–Chilean alliance against Pincheira tenuous at best. In actuality, the state's strength in numbers belied vulnerability and weakness. Even though Beauchef managed to disperse some members of Pincheira's band and take valuable cattle and goods, the core remained intact for another five years. Even the caciques, "who said they would hand over Pincheira during the winter,"[70] did not succeed in doing so.

Second, Beauchef's expedition illustrates the Pincheira brothers' power and control over the region. By seeking help from the Trapatrapa Pehuenches, Beauchef hoped to increase friction between the two Pehuenche groups in favor of the state. His strategy worked briefly, but his failure to capture Pincheira left the Trapatrapa Pehuenches vulnerable to Pincheira's wrath once he left the area in the winter, as had happened on previous occasions.[71]

Lastly, Beauchef's expedition reflects his—and by extension the state's—general attitude toward the indigenous population. Beauchef and his commanders sought aid from the Trapatrapa Pehuenches to capture Pincheira, but according to his memoirs, he spared no expense in debasing those same Pehuenches whose help he was seeking. For example, while waiting to hear from Levimanque and his nephew, he stated, "In general, the Pehuenche Indians are very lazy and cowardly."[72] Once Levimanque agreed to follow him, Beauchef wrote:

> I made them understand that we were not barbarians like those who accompanied Pincheira, who would disembowel their friends and neighbors without remorse. That we had other ideas with respect to youth and the fatality of the bad example they had received from their parents. That once you have left these villains, you will have learned the virtues of humanity and religion that prohibits men from being cruel to their fellow men. That without doubt, their mothers would have taught them some ideas concerning the punishments that await in the other life of one who misbehaves, and that there they would not have escaped.[73]

Moreover, there was another, much darker side to Beauchef's statements. The words, the gifts such as aguardiente, and the offers formed part of the state's larger strategy to enlist Mapuche support in its plans to subjugate Araucanía. But its inability to contain the Pincheira–Pehuenche threat throughout the 1820s increased the chaos and instability in the region.

The continued guerrilla war in Araucanía forced the newly formed republic to use its resources in Araucanía, neglecting the capital. Problems in the capital, however, impeded the prompt arrival of supplies and troops in Araucanía, where they were in short supply. The police in Santiago bitterly argued this exact point in a public governmental document released as a newspaper on April 28, 1827:

> The police need funds. The Nation has not declared itself according to the form of government it has chosen and without this the basic principles of the police force may not be resolved; she [the police] is the daughter of the administration and as such will continue her own march. . . . Chile will not be able to have her if it continues to establish itself through a unitarian or federal form of government. While this provisional state continues to exist, the police cannot, nor should it do more than guard order and prevent those customs and abuses that universal opinion dictates.[74]

The civil war of 1829–1830 exacerbated the existing political and military problems. Generals Joaquín Prieto and Ramón Freire, who believed they had eliminated the royalist threat in Araucanía, now found themselves fighting against each other. After Prieto's win, he eradicated all previous liberal experiments, including the 1828 constitution.

For the next three years, the victorious conservative government worked to consolidate state power in the young republic. Yet Araucanía remained a problem. Royalists such as Benavides and Pico no longer threatened the state, but the Mapuche took full advantage of the state's continued military disorganization in Araucanía to pursue their own political agendas, a topic discussed in detail in chapters 4 and 5. Guerrilla warfare in the south ceased for two decades with the capture of José Antonio Pincheira in 1832, marking the beginning of the state's firm grip over Araucanía. With the ratification of the 1833 constitution, political infighting in Santiago ended, and the conservative administrations now in control of the state focused their considerable military and economic resources on the eventual subjugation of Araucanía and its Mapuche inhabitants.

The 1833 Constitution

The political chaos during the 1820s created numerous problems for the Chilean state. The continuing conflicts in Araucanía only increased the political instability that plagued Chile's leaders during this period. The conservative victory at the Battle of Lircay ushered in a new period in Chilean history called "the Portalian years,"[75] after Diego Portales, who dominated the political scene during the early 1830s. Although Portales was never president, his influence with the ruling class was extensive. In the late 1820s and early 1830s, he held several ministerial posts to disseminate his political ideas. According to one historian, his disdain for leadership on a direct level did not affect his ability to "rule Chile in league with [Joaquín] Prieto, Prieto's nephew, Manuel Bulnes, and Manuel Rengifo, who became minister of finance."[76] Portales believed that liberalism, democracy, and popular suffrage were incapable of producing a stable society and that Chile was in need of a political overhaul to create "viable national political institutions through which to govern effectively and stimulate economic recovery."[77]

Portales, minister of the interior at the time, relied on his aristocratic background to influence the government from behind the scenes. Born in 1793 to don Santiago Portales and doña María Fernández de Palazuelo, Diego Portales was descended from one of the oldest Chilean aristocratic families. He studied humanities and law but grew tired of both disciplines and became a businessman. He married young, but his wife died soon thereafter. Alone, he spent two years in Peru, where many of his political ideas took shape. In 1823 Portales's company, Portales and Cea, brokered a ten-year monopoly deal with the state (the estanco) on the sale of tobacco, tea, liquor, and cards, which fell apart in 1826. Through his company's contract with the state, Portales expanded his conservative power base and influenced many people in government and business.

With the defeat of the pipiolos at the Battle of Lircay, the pelucones asked Portales to help establish a new government. In 1830 Vice President José Tomás Ovalle, a good friend of Portales's, became president. The path was set for Portales to carry out his political ambitions for Chile.[78] The cornerstones of Portales's policies were order and stability: "One strong hand and only one was the answer to the governing of the newly born nations of the New Continent."[79] He believed in the rule of law, with the important caveat that the political situation had to be normal.[80] In other words, "When there are sufficient motives, when the future of the state is at stake, not only can the laws and constitution be broken, they must be."[81] For Portales, then, laws were for the country, not the other way around. One historian described Portales as someone who "commanded respect from his political enemies and planned to organize the administration of the state in a manner not seen previously."[82]

After the pelucones consolidated their political hold on the nation in 1830, Portales's first goal was to end the guerrilla warfare in Araucanía. In 1831 he engineered several laws to combat the large number of crimes committed in the republic. Less than a year later, the subject of increasing crime rates appeared in the newspaper *El Araucano* when the district attorney wrote a letter to the supreme court, lamenting "that crime is increasing in a horrible progression, and the nation is on the road to moral ruin; and it cannot be any other way if one considers the impunity that the criminals receive, and that outside the capital there is no punishment that may be applied or else it is the punishment that is decreed (if not eluded altogether) late and so distant from the theater of crime that no lesson is being taught."[83]

Portales formed a government that he believed abided by the rule of law, and he criticized the transitional government's blunders. For example, in a letter to his friend don Antonio Garfias in April 1832, he expressed his disgust over the government's formation of a military unit whose captain, Francisco Rojas, had been a commander in Pincheira's montonera.[84] "It would be very difficult for the Government to do anything more scandalous, idiotic, immoral and impolitic: the soldiers that will make-up the Company are without a doubt the same ones as Pincheira's. . . . What discipline, what order, what subordination will there be with these licentious people whose vices are already established? What will the morale of the public and most of all that of the Army be, when they see the robberies and assassinations of so many years being rewarded?"[85] Portales suggested that his friend let the ministry in charge know of this grievous error and disband this military unit.

In Portales's view of the world, there was no room for ex-bandits and criminals, especially those who in Portales's eyes escaped punishment. In the same letter, he mentions how these soldiers, whom he facetiously terms "family," will "provoke the natives into war and then will rob them and the whole world!"[86] His distrust of anyone who had any involvement with Pincheira reflects just how much of a threat Pincheira had been to the state. Having an ex-officer of Pincheira command a corps of soldiers in Araucanía potentially set the stage for further conflicts in that region, a situation Portales wanted to avoid.

Portales's crowning achievement was the 1833 constitution. Although he was not a formal author of the constitution, the document contained many of his political ideas and ambitions. In the spring of 1831, a constituent assembly gathered to reform the 1828 constitution. The same assembly reconvened in October 1832 and examined several drafts. Mariano Egaña, Juan Egaña's son, submitted the most influential of these drafts, which with several omissions became the new constitution in May 1833. Portales did not attend any of these constitutional assemblies.[87]

The 1833 constitution differed significantly from Chile's previous ones. It placed enormous emphasis on the presidency, allowing the president to have two consecutive five-year terms and considerable power over the other branches of government (chapters VI and VII).[88] It also gave the president the ability to issue regulations and instructions to the rest of the government: "To the President of the Republic is conferred the administration and government of the State; and his authority extends to all that is necessary to maintain public order in the interior, and the external security of the Republic, guarding the Constitution and the law."[89] The president also could veto any existing legislation without the possibility of the congress reconsidering it in the present session,[90] and the president could declare a state of siege,[91] which happened several times after 1833.[92]

Suffrage requirements included literacy and property ownership, a major change from the 1828 constitution.[93] In this respect, the 1833 charter was more like the 1823 constitution. Unlike in previous governments, however, the lax enforcement and "deliberate delays [of the literacy requirement] . . . allowed landowners to enroll their tenants as voters and militia commanders to do likewise with their troops, making it easier to manipulate elections in favor of the existing government and effectively blocking any opposition."[94] General Prieto called this system, and the 1833 constitution, "a means of putting an end to the revolutions and disturbances which arose from the confusion in which the triumph of independence left us."[95]

The combination of a strong presidency with expanded powers and limited suffrage created a powerful tool for a state determined to eliminate the chaos of the 1820s and to achieve an orderly and moral society. It also created an autocratic system of government, with few rights and liberties for the average citizen. Previous administrations had attempted to accomplish these same objectives since the 1823 constitution. What made the 1833 constitution so successful, however, was precisely the centralization of political power within the governing elite and the end of guerrilla warfare in Araucanía.

Portales at first thought the constitution did not provide sufficient emphasis on law and order: "One cannot come to terms with men of law; for what devil of a purpose serve Constitutions and bits of paper if they are not capable of remedying a known problem, or one that is going to occur . . . by taking the measures needed to end them. . . . This respect for delinquents, or suspected delinquents will finish the country rapidly. . . . I know how to say, with the law or without it, this lady called the Constitution must be violated when the circumstances are extreme."[96] Peace and prosperity returned to Chile after 1833, but it did so under a repressive constitution and in an atmosphere that, at least on the surface, maintained an artificially prescribed order.

Conclusion

Portales's and, by extension, the state's concerns about morality and order were a reaction to events in Araucanía. Throughout the 1820s, the various national governments made repeated attempts to eliminate the Pincheira montonera. These efforts severely stressed the state's resources and created difficult political problems that resulted in a civil war. Furthermore, the state's inability to control events in Araucanía, together with political wrangling in Santiago, impeded Chile's leaders from implementing a program of law and order in their state-building project. With the restoration of order on the political front and Pincheira's capture, Portales initiated his and, by extension, the state's political plan of action for the new republic, which ultimately became the 1833 constitution. What was the Pincheira montonera and how did it come into existence? Who headed the montonera? What was its purpose? I suggest answers to these questions in the next chapter.

CHAPTER THREE

"Enemies" of the State

The Pincheira Montonera

FOR TWELVE YEARS, the Pincheira brothers and their men raided, looted, pillaged, and stole cattle and women from the local haciendas in Araucanía. Their raids also extended as far north as the province of Mendoza on the eastern side of the Andes. So potent were the Pincheira *malones* (raids) that even a hint of their presence was enough to frighten people away, as the following soldier's description aptly illustrates:

> On the eleventh, at the hour at which I was to begin marching with
> my party, I heard discharges from the plaza, and a soldier, forgetting
> his interests and even the mother who gave birth to him, believed that
> Pincheira had just attacked the quarter. At that moment, I decided to flee
> by the back of a building and just as I thought about finding myself head-
> to-head with the bandits, I saw the national flag hanging on the front of
> the houses. The sight of the flags as well as the sounds of bells quieted my
> unruly spirit, returning my breath that had escaped me while fleeing.[1]

The Chilean state viewed the Pincheira brothers as traitors and enemies of the state because they were royalists who supported the Spanish crown. The state also considered them bandits because they were breaking the law. As royalists, the Pincheiras threatened the Chilean state's newly won independence, and as bandits, they threatened the state's ability to exist in an atmosphere of law and order.

Bandits, regardless of their classification, share a certain degree of power over the elite and members of their own class, expressed through a variety of means (extortion, blackmail, robbery, killing of prominent members in government who stand in their way, and so on). Bandits' ability to wield power over others may attract popular support in the form of safe havens from authorities or a supply of contraband goods,[2] but this support is limited because of the fear bandits instill in their supporters. Nonetheless, people benefit from bandit activities because bandits often provide local townspeople protection and give them gifts for services rendered. Bandits routinely utilize their position as outlaws as a form of protest against the state's repressive authority and gain popular support for their activities. This contrasts with common criminals, who not only are outcasts of society but also do not have a base of support because their activities are illegal and no one benefits from them except the criminals themselves. The Pincheira brothers were political bandits who fought against the Chilean state to maintain their lucrative hold on trade with the Mapuche. They were indeed members of society, not outsiders. What made the Pincheira brothers such a threat to the newly formed Chilean state, however, was their power over a large geographic region that had since colonial times largely been autonomous from any central authority, including the Spanish crown. The Pincheira's relationship with the powerful Pehuenches, and their network of support from local communities, further strengthened their power base. Nevertheless, their actions did not necessarily benefit the local communities, since they did not discriminate among the latifundias and towns they raided. They were thus not social bandits but rather political bandits, whose allegiance to the Spanish crown (whether real or feigned) made them traitors to independence and to the Chilean Republic.[3] In fact, the Pincheiras' actions and the local support they received from indigenous as well as white communities made them more like Indians than bandits. Yet the state made a distinction between the Pincheiras and their Mapuche allies. Even though they were most likely mestizos, the state did not consider them to be Indians, even if they acted as such. The Pincheiras were bandits, however, because they threatened the political stability of a fragile, newly created state.

This chapter discusses the history of the celebrated Pincheiras through an examination of their exploits, their alliances with Pehuenches, and the Chilean state's reactions to their activities. It is important to stress that the

Pincheiras were not a mere nuisance to the Chilean state. Their allegiance to the Spanish crown and alliance with a powerful indigenous group posed a serious problem for the state formation during this chaotic period. The state's inability to stop them early and quickly attests to the Pincheiras' tenacity and perhaps determination to pursue their own goals in this new society. The ultimate dissolution of the Pincheira montonera in March 1832 allowed the state to initiate a new strategic plan that culminated in the 1833 constitution, discussed in the previous chapter. However, this new plan of action could not have taken place before the montonera's disbandment.

The Pincheira Brothers

There were four Pincheira brothers, but the two youngest, Pablo and José Antonio, were the most important. The Pincheira brothers worked as inquilinos at the Hacienda of Cato, in the district of Chillán. Their father, Martín, was an inquilino in the same hacienda. Antonio, the eldest, founded the montonera after deserting the royalist forces at the Battle of Chacabuco in 1817. He died from a stray bullet during a raid on Linares on April 26, 1823. Santos, the third brother, also died in the 1820s. In a letter to Benjamín Vicuña Mackenna dated June 2, 1868, Bernardo Villagram, a one-time follower of Pincheira, provided him with a little bit of Pincheira history: "Santos was a good man who never accompanied his brothers on their excursions; he occupied himself with raising cattle or in diplomatic missions concerning the Indians and in one of those trips he drowned in the big river."[4] Pablo became the leader of the montonera when his brother Antonio died in 1823. His younger brother, José Antonio, took command sometime in 1826. Under Pablo's guidance, the montonera gained its reputation for barbarism and cruelty. Pablo instilled fear into the hearts of his men as well as in anyone who crossed his path. A prominent nineteenth-century historian describes Pablo as "adventurous by instinct, daring and astute and an expert in all forms of vices."[5] Early on "he committed many robberies and other graver crimes that attracted his persecution under the law and effectively made him an outlaw."[6] Another historian describes him as "the most ferocious and villainous of the Pincheira brothers. He was the type of vulgar robber, who besides being cruel was a coward."[7] There is evidence that he did not accept criticism from members of his band and that his one remaining brother was not fond of him.[8] Pablo died in a skirmish with federal troops in January 1832.

José Antonio's leadership was the exact opposite of his brother Pablo's. Like his elder brother Santos, he was known as a relatively peaceful man.[9] Throughout his tenure as leader of the montonera, he maintained a close working relationship with his allies, the Pehuenches, and treated his men with respect.[10] He surrendered in March 1832, received a pardon from the state, and lived the rest of his long life by the Ñuble River.[11]

From 1819 to 1832, the Pincheira brothers and their Pehuenche allies conducted malones on the frontier, burning haciendas, rustling cattle, and capturing women, whom they would keep as concubines for the men. A priest named Padre Gómez forced all men who kept women, including Pehuenches, to get married.[12] Whether all women married or not is not clear, but the Pincheiras maintained a seminomadic existence, with camps high up in the cordillera on the outskirts of the central-southern city of Chillán. Their central camp was near the lakes of Epulafquen, a desolate and nearly impassable area fondly named la Montaña. Here the Pincheiras carried the booty from their raids in the summer and fall, and set up camp for the winter. Once the winter snow thawed in the spring, they started the process again. Their raids were frequent and deadly, and the state often lost. For example, in December 1825, Juan de Dios Rivera, then senior minister of the War Department, related,

> The denaturalized Pincheira has been put in retreat after the battle that took place November 27th against the Villa of Parral, whose antecedents I wrote about in Dispatch No. 62 on that same day. His forces were too much for our men and resulted in the death of 52 dragoons. Nonetheless, the enemy's loss was not inferior. Cacique Carripil, principal fomenter of this war ended up a cadaver. Commander of the division in the North, Coronel Don Domingo Torres chased after them but probably without much results because of the inferiority of his horses. Jordán's valiant corps received 130 lance injuries; such is the ferocity of these miscreants, that even when a man is dead there is no security from their fury![13]

On another occasion, "a party of 200 men invaded Curicó, the capital of the province of Colchagua, and although immediately a similar number of peasants and militiamen on horseback were organized to attack them, they were defeated; in their escape eight were killed and many others were left injured; the bandits have sacked various haciendas, and finally retreated, leaving terror, tears, and anxiety among the defenseless inhabitants."[14] For much of the 1820s the Pincheiras' montonera was successful in its malones, selling the cattle and other stolen goods to Mapuche allies on the Chilean as well as the Argentine side of the cordillera, and gaining considerable profit in the process. Aside from earning a profit, the Pincheira montonera also maintained an allegiance to the Spanish crown, a threat to the newly established Chilean Republic.

The Pincheiras' allegiance to the Spanish crown is significant for several reasons. First, the area of Chillán was a hotbed of royalist tendencies during the independence wars (1810–1824) and home of the Colegio de Propaganda Fide de Chillán. The school, located in the cordillera foothills near the town of Santa Barbara, acted as a mission where children of Pehuenche caciques, as well as residents of Chillán, were educated and received instruction in the Catholic faith. It also enjoyed a reputation for its "fervent support of the [Spanish] king," which the Franciscan friars utilized well.[15] These friars educated many sons of caciques, including two sons of Cacique Francisco Mariluán, discussed in the next chapter. Because of the colegio's strategic location and extensive contact with Pehuenches, it is likely that many of the latter received instruction from the Franciscan friars. "Although they [the Franciscans] were not able to convert them to Catholicism, they at least had political influence, and on this occasion, they knew how to utilize it."[16] Their mission in Chillán and the surrounding communities included the teaching of royalism. The Pincheiras' loyalty to the Spanish crown can thus be more easily explained in light of their relationship with Pehuenches who had close ties to this school.

Because of the constant royalist conspiracy and agitation against Creole forces, Bernardo O'Higgins ordered the school closed in 1817. After the civil war of 1829–1830, however, the pelucón government decided to reopen the doors of the Colegio de Propaganda Fide de Chillán as a "tool for the pacification of the frontier area and as a center for reducing and civilizing the Indians in the area."[17] The official decree reopening the school read, "The principal object of its establishment, it said in Article 3, is to send missionaries among the barbarous Indians to initiate them in the principles of our sacred religion, and to procure their civilization, and to sustain a school in its convent for the young Indians who want to come and receive an education."[18] After considerable debate concerning the reopening of the school, the state decided to staff it with young religious people to avoid any further problems. In 1832 the Spanish were no longer a threat, so the state felt comfortable reopening the school.

During the early days of their struggle with the Chilean state, the Pincheiras were royalists because it meant opposition to a state of which they did not want to be a part. In 1817 the eldest brother, Antonio, for unknown reasons, became disillusioned with the prospects of a new nation and turned to banditry to escape capture from creole forces. He founded the montonera, and by the early 1820s he and his brothers had amassed a large membership that varied in size as well as background: "There were in Pincheira's montonera men of diverse backgrounds: Spaniards, men from Mendoza, men from Córdoba; but the most numerous were the Chileans, principally from the region of Chillán. There was one occasion when they reached 700 in number; but when they surrendered they were no more than 270: the rest had died or had returned to their homes."[19] In a letter to the governor intendant of Concepción dated April 30, 1819, the commander of San Carlos, Justo Muñóz, claims that "he [Pincheira] has hundreds of men fully armed" and that "they with their Pehuenche allies will always have us on the move."[20]

For the Pincheiras and their Pehuenche allies, rather than an actual ideology, royalism was a general political strategy of opposition to an organized state that interfered with their commercial activities. For example, the brothers' military alliance with pelucón general Joaquín Prieto during the 1829 civil war demonstrates their capacity to align with anyone—regardless of political ideology—who was willing to support their economic activities. The Pincheiras and their Pehuenche allies provided General Prieto's troops passage through unknown and difficult terrain in the south, a pipiolo stronghold. In exchange, Pincheira's band was not harassed, infuriating the British consul of Concepción, Henry William Rouse, who saw the Pincheiras as mere criminals and complained to the Earl of Aberdeen: "A general trusted with a military force to repress the inroads of a band of merciless assassins should not merely abandon his post and turn his arms against the state; but degrade himself so far as to be the first to call in those assassins to aid in proclaiming the criminality of his enterprise."[21] Upon winning the civil war in 1830, General Prieto increased his efforts at capturing the Pincheiras and their Pehuenche allies, who had been given de facto amnesty during the war and were now once again considered enemies of the state.

Countless skirmishes between the Pincheiras, their Pehuenche and Spanish allies, and the Chilean army serve as examples of the Pincheiras' royalism during these years. One incident took place in San Carlos on May 20, 1820. Justo Muñóz related the following in a letter to the governor intendant of Concepción: "With the rising of the sun this morning the Enemy, with 200 armed men has invaded this Town. Its commanders were Pincheyra [sic] . . . ; they didn't suffer more than a few discharges before they fled. In the struggle, we managed to take a prisoner who is from this area and who declared that only two Pehuenches were with them. We have not continued our pursuit due to the small numbers in our force. We have requested reinforcements from Chillán in order to pursue them."[22] On another occasion Pedro Barnachea, commander of the frontier, wrote to his superior, "According to what I have heard Pico and Pincheira have raided from points north. I know where they were camped, and if fortune allows me, will give them their final extermination. In this intelligence, I'm considering an excursion with a party of considerable number upon them; which would be composed of those that are in Trapa-Trapa and forces taken from this division and united with those of Commander Bulnes, if you Sir, have him return to us."[23]

According to one historian, it was in 1825, when a Spanish captain named Miguel de Sinosiain joined the montonera, that the Pincheiras became royalists. He claims that aside from supplies and arms, Sinosiain also provided the Pincheiras with other "benefits that were a thousand times more valuable, that they had previously not had; they were in the service of a cause and the defense of a flag."[24] Until that point "the Pincheiras had been horrible bandits without much of a cause other than robbery, and assault, without any other flag than that of pillage and desolation."[25] Given the abundance of evidence about the Pincheiras' royalist tendencies since 1819, including their own letters, it seems very probable that the Pincheiras had been royalists all along. For instance, in 1823 Pablo Pincheira wrote,

Sir . . . I have received your appreciable note in which you invite me and

my men to surrender with a full pardon, that until this time I have had
the honor of commanding in order to defend the sacred arms of both
Majesties, not because I have received any title but because I have arrived
from the air. . . . During this year I thought I would have a final assault
and then go to Buenos Aires with all of my troops and there receive
a pardon from the Viceroy . . . and I know he will receive me. . . . to
Coronel Clemente Lantaño.[26]

There is evidence that tensions existed between Pablo and his younger
brother, José Antonio, concerning the future of the montonera and their
ongoing allegiance to the Spanish crown. A month earlier, José Antonio
began treaty negotiations with Colonel Clemente Lantaño, without Pablo's
consent. Upon finding out, Pablo refused to negotiate any treaties and, to
prove a point, looted several latifundias in the town of San Carlos. A letter
from Juan de Dios Rivera confirms this: "The negotiations between Coronel Clemente Lantaño and one of the Pincheiras was destroyed by his
brother, who did not want to enter into any treaties, after he was informed
of what the government would offer. As a consequence, this treacherous
brother made an exit through San Carlos, attacking several haciendas in
his escape. Because of the ineptitude of the Commander in charge, over
twenty men from the San Carlos militias and an officer of the militia in
Quirihue died."[27]

Pablo continued to fight under the royalist banner because *royalist* was the
only political label that effectively opposed an independent state during this
period in Chile. It is not clear why José Antonio seemed ready to deal with
the state in 1823. No treaty between the Pincheiras and the state took place
that year, and José Antonio continued to serve as second-in-command under
Pablo. The continuing conflicts between the brothers, nonetheless, cost
Pablo his leadership position three years later.

Another explanation for the Pincheiras' royalist support was their long-
time relationship with the Pehuenches. Like other Mapuche groups, the
Pehuenches opposed the Chilean state because they respected the various
parlamentos that had been held with Spanish authorities since colonial
times, by which Araucanía remained a separate, independent entity. For the
Pehuenches, then, being royalist was part of a continuous discourse of independence from and struggle against an encroaching Chilean state that was

very different from a crown that had previously acknowledged their independent territory. Their alliance with the Pincheira brothers was mutually beneficial. The Pincheiras protected the Pehuenches from land-hungry Chileans in exchange for safe access through Pehuenche territory and protection from the Chilean army.

Royalist support was also intricately linked to their commercial interests. The Pincheiras and Pehuenches traded cattle to other Mapuche groups and trained the horses for future malones. The Pincheiras also exchanged goods with the Pehuenches, usually in return for access into and through Pehuenche territory. For their part, the Pehuenches provided the Pincheiras with protection from the Chilean army, either physically or through a network of spies who alerted them of the army's presence in their area of operations. In 1823 Juan de Dios Rivera, the governor intendant of Concepción, wrote a letter to his superior, Pedro Barnachea, the commander of the army on the frontier. In it Rivera warned Barnachea to keep quiet a detailed plan to ambush Pincheira at the lagoons near Tucapel, in the foothills of the cordillera, for fear of having the information leaked to Pincheira: "And among themselves Caciques Pintuntin and Campil are those that are sustaining Pincheira, . . . thus we make haste to accost this miscreant [Pincheira] . . . it should not be told to anyone, for now, because they communicate any little detail to Pincheira through Chillán and San Carlos."[28]

The relationship between the Pincheiras and Pehuenches, although mutually beneficial, was not equal. Pehuenches who failed to cooperate with the Pincheiras found their trade goods and possessions taken or destroyed, and their commercial activities disrupted. In one letter Pedro Barnachea explained that "several caciques no longer wanted to ally with the Pincheiras because they were disrupting the caciques' commercial activities in the region."[29] The Pehuenches respected the power of the Pincheiras and frequently misled army troops.

Although the Pincheira brothers often acted much like their Pehuenche allies, the Chilean state did not consider them Indians. State officials repeatedly distinguished between the Indians and the Pincheiras, often referring to the latter as *bandidos* and *enemigos*. In a letter to Pedro Barnachea, Juan de Dios Rivera writes, "the villainous Pincheiras cannot be destroyed without penetrating their security forces: Coronel Lantaño proposes a plan to use some of his own militia to go after this horde of criminals."[30] Further, "Being

it now necessary to work against the banditry perpetuated by this unnatural-
ized Pincheira, please keep me informed of his particulars."[31]

On the other hand, the state always identified the Mapuche as Indians,
with distinctions made as to whether they were friendly or enemy Indians.
For example, in a letter to Barnachea on March 5, 1826, Rivera talks about
"Faustina Saez [who] has brought me the news that the enemy Indians and
their allies have reunited in Tratrapa."[32] Regardless of the terminology the
state utilized to distinguish the Pincheiras from the Mapuche (including the
Pehuenches), the state considered both the Pincheiras and their Pehuenche
allies enemies. Additionally, the trade network the Pincheiras and Pehuenches managed with other Mapuche groups was outside of state control,
and the Pincheira montonera's allegiance to the Spanish crown, which their
Pehuenche allies shared, posed a political threat to the state. In a very real
sense, then, the state's push to control Araucanía and its inhabitants to further the economic and political process of state formation hinged entirely on
the need to destroy the Pincheira montonera.

For the Pincheiras, their allegiance to the king of Spain was a symbolic
act of defiance but simultaneously an act of resistance to an established
order with which they did not agree, and one that severely restricted their
economic activities with the Mapuche communities on both sides of the
cordillera, such as when the state convinced a group of Indians to "send
fifty men to Pincheiras' stronghold to impede trade with him."[33] For the
brothers, then, the state was the traitor because it had broken away from
the Spanish crown. They, as subjects of the Spanish state, had to defend
the crown. They did so by conducting raids and harassing army soldiers.
They remained royalist because they received support from Pico, Hermosilla, and Sinosiain, royalist commanders who still operated in Araucanía and for a brief period had troops and supplies to continue the war.
After Pico's death, the Pincheiras still fought under the banner of royalism,
but they did so to protect their trade activities. What at first may have been
truly an allegiance to an ideological cause became a profitable venture
whereby the Pincheira brothers gained considerable economic profits and
power. Local support from influential people who sent the Pincheiras letters via spies attests to their influence, especially in the Chillán area.[34]

Relationships with the Local Community

Local support for the Pincheiras existed as early as 1818, when the montonera was in its infancy. In his *Historia Jeneral de Chile*, Diego Barros Arana mentioned a doña Cruz Arran of Chillán, who "provided the best services to the Pincheira band."[35] In a letter to the editor of *El Verdadero Liberal*, a concerned citizen wrote that a "Manuel Zañartu supported the Pincheira montonera by buying him lances and, furthermore, according to Clemente Lantaño [a Pincheira supporter], he asserts that he received money from Pincheira to buy clothes for his prisoners."[36] Aside from spontaneous local support, the Pincheira montonera's effectiveness stemmed from its relationship with influential community members, including hacendados and a well-informed network of spies. Spies—anyone from merchants to members of the montonera—were critical to the success of the Pincheira malones.

There were at least three court cases against spies reputed to work for the Pincheira brothers.[37] In one, a spy named José María Betancur confessed to his captors that he had worked for the Pincheiras for six years and that his main job consisted of tracking the Chilean state's military movements at various points, which he then relayed to the Pincheiras through a series of signals: "He would signal six other men by making a fire."[38] It was while he was making one of these fires that some of General Freire's men captured him in February 1826. The trial transcript reveals how connected some members of the local community were to the Pincheira band. For example, Betancur confessed that "a Don Pedro Sepúlveda supplies provisions and that so does a Don José, brother of Longaví [a local hacendado]."[39]

In another spy case, the accused, José María Concha, a twenty-five-year-old merchant and native of Mendoza, Argentina, confessed that he had met Pincheira in July 1829 when his government in Mendoza had made a deal with Pincheira, although he did not specify the contents of the deal. In the summary of the trial, the government accused Concha of spying for Pincheira and of "interpreting the language of the Indians."[40] Arrested with Concha was Cecilio Tofre, a native of San Juan, Argentina. In his confession, Tofre related that he had left his country to find work, that he had known Concha for three months, that Concha was a merchant who worked with Pincheira, and that he (Concha) had been in prison in Mendoza because he had goods and slaves that were not allowed in Mendoza. He also confessed that Concha had a nephew who was a member of Pincheira's band, a claim that is substantiated in the summary of the trial: "And more, [Concha] is the uncle of one of the commanders of [Pincheira]."[41] Tofre also substantiated the government's claim that Concha acted as an interpreter for the Indians when he confessed that "he too knows the language of the Pehuenches because he has heard him speak and sing in the said language."[42]

These spies were from Argentina, illustrating that Pincheira's influence reached beyond the borders of Chile. Also clear from Concha's case is that Pincheira had commercial dealings with him. Furthermore, these commercial activities took place not only in Mendoza but also on the Chilean side of the border. They also involved Mapuches, as evidenced by Concha's language skills. Concha's relationship with Pincheira is significant because, besides being a merchant and spy, he acted as an intermediary for the Indians associated with Pincheira. The Concha case signifies that Pincheira did not rely just on local patronage for support but rather exercised his influence over a wide geographical area. Without this patronage, which provided key supplies and political support to the Pincheira band, their activities would have been much more difficult to sustain. The Pincheiras' dominance beyond the Chilean border also made it more difficult for the Chilean army to capture them.

The Mendoza Treaty

On July 15, 1829, José Antonio Pincheira, together with the Spaniard Julian Hermosilla and others in his montonera, made a pact with the governor of the province of Mendoza. The treaty, among other things, made José Antonio Pincheira "the head of the unit of the South"[43] and authorized Pincheira to "defend the province with which he had sought an agreement and he agreed to complete any orders given to him by the said government of the province."[44] Article 5, however, differs significantly: "If the province of Mendoza initiates a war with the Republic of Chile, the force of said general is not obligated to fight unless it is for defensive purposes only."[45] Here Pincheira admitted not only that Chile was a republic but also that he was willing to fight for Mendoza only if it was defending itself from an aggressive act on the part of Chile. Otherwise, he reserved the right to abstain from interfering. This observation is interesting in light of Pincheira's prior political allegiance to Spain, which did not recognize Chile as a republic. In fact, Pincheira claimed to be fighting for the Spanish flag the entire decade of the 1820s. Pincheira's statement in the Mendoza Treaty is another example of his use of political labels to suit his particular goals at the time. During the 1820s, opposition to an organized state came under the banner of royalism. By the end of the decade, the term had little significance, since Chile had won independence and the new nation-state had eliminated any remnants of the Spanish crown. Thus Pincheira had little choice but to adopt a new political stance for his activities by becoming a de facto commander of Mendoza Province.

El Valdiviano Federal published the treaty in August 1829, with accompanying opinion pieces pertaining to a competing newspaper's (*La Clave*) treatment of the treaty. In one opinion piece, the author actually congratulated Pincheira for his actions with the province of Mendoza, since he now no longer pillaged and terrorized people on the Chilean side of the border. As he put it, "All Chileans will look upon this with pleasure since that agreement will secure life and property which was impossible under the bayonets that with enormous waste from our treasury, were annually sent to defend them."[46]

Even more significant than the actual treaty was the timing, which coincided directly with the civil war between the pipiolos and pelucones, in which Pincheira's montonera assisted the pelucón side by providing access through difficult mountainous terrain and enhancing Prieto's superiority over the pipiolos. The pelucones' victory in 1830 changed the political landscape, however, and even though Pincheira had provided critical aid to General Prieto, Chile's new pelucón leaders denied his aid and renewed their efforts at capturing him.

Pincheira's treaty with the governor of Mendoza in July 1829 was a political statement as well as a safety net. From Mendoza, Pincheira was able to consolidate his dwindling montonera and regroup for further malones on Chilean soil. An article in the Santiago newspaper *El Araucano* on January 8, 1831, announced his return to Chile: "This man, formidable because of the position he has, and pernicious because of the ruin he leaves in his path, maintains himself camped on the western end of the cordillera, in front of the city of Chillán and he has a force of men whom he sends out in small parties to commit atrocities."[47] The article further elaborates on Pincheira's behavior by mentioning an incident whereby "two of his officers, Rojas and Hermosilla, made an excursion in front of Talca, which they effectively did, taking with them about one thousand head of cattle, including cows, horses and mules from the haciendas adjacent to the cordillera."[48] The army was ill-equipped to pursue the montonera: "It was not possible to prevent this disaster, because the mobility of the bandits is no match for our army. When the Commander of the Cantón in Maule heard the news, he dispatched a group of cavalry and two infantry parties. And although these brave men pursued them in great haste, they were not able to catch them because the passage through this area was inaccessible."[49]

In January 1831, don Claudio Gay was on a traveling mission for the state in Araucanía and almost became a victim of the Pincheiras. He described his experience: "On January 4, 1831, while alerting the government of the bandits in the area, I found myself in the cordillera, and I had passed the night in los Chacayes, near the confluence of the Cipreces River with the Cachapoal River. Mid-morning, some of my men who had stayed in Chacayes, on the other side of the river, noticed some individuals dressed as shepherds and assuming they were servants of the hacienda Compañía, invited them for a drink of *mate* [herbal tea]. And thus, it was that members of Pincheira's band came in disguise."[50]

The bandits left him alone and he arrived at his destination without incident: "They left without any malice or taking anything, without doubt aware of the fear they inspired. Given notice of this incident, I climbed the mountains and after two days I was able to arrive near the baths at Cauquenes where I found a militia company in hot pursuit of the bandits who, of course, had already made it to their camp."[51] One month later, while on a trip to the volcano of Talcarehue, "however, the fear they instilled in San Fernando . . . was so great that my attempted visit to the volcano of Talcarehue could only be accomplished with a military escort under the orders of Intendant, Pedro Urriola."[52]

In the last months of 1830 and the first months of 1831, Pincheira "renewed his endeavors with greater insolence and temerity . . . in order to snatch the cattle they found in the countryside, killing innocent workers who attempted to resist them and taking captive any women and children they found in their way."[53] The state's attempts at capturing and prosecuting the montonera failed. "The troops sent after them, not only were not able to catch them but barely managed to save some of the stolen cattle that the bandits were forced to leave in their escape."[54]

To prevent more failures and to fortify their new position, in 1832 the pelucones appointed General Manuel Bulnes, a hero of the independence wars and future president of Chile, to pursue and demolish the Pincheira montonera. General Bulnes was no stranger to Araucanía, and through his efforts José Antonio Pincheira finally surrendered a few months later. The events leading up to his final surrender made headlines in several newspapers. *Documentos Oficiales* recounted one of Pincheira's last battles, in January 1832, where his brother Pablo and several important caciques died: "Yesterday the fourteenth of the present month, after many violent marches and immense difficulties in traveling through the arid and elevated cordillera, I arrived at two in the morning to this position with three formidable columns that formed the army under my command, who immediately began to disseminate my orders and has reduced to nothing the horde of bandits that were camped here, and united with the barbarous Pehuenche natives."[55] *El Araucano* ran several stories in the first few months of 1832, chronicling Pincheira's last malón and his subsequent escape and eventual capture. They make for high drama. On January 16, 1832, a party under the command of Bulnes attacked Pincheira's camp in Las Lagunas. The principal casualties were Pablo Pincheira, Hermosilla, and a few others.[56] Although the state claimed that it had essentially destroyed the bandit gang, José Antonio escaped with several of his men. Nonetheless, the death of his brother Pablo was a severe setback for him, and he surrendered to the state two months later. Under an agreement reached with General Bulnes, he turned himself in to Pedro Lavanderos, one of his former officers, on the condition that the state spare his life. General Bulnes agreed, and José Antonio Pincheira surrendered in Chillán on March 11, 1832.[57]

The above analysis of the Pincheira montonera refutes long-standing notions that they were simple bandits. One historian claims that the Pincheiras were not able "to transform themselves into a rebellion or social revolution because of their limited social objectives."[58] In contrast, the Pincheiras did indeed lead a rebellion of sorts. Through their evolving political allegiances and actions, they provoked a response from a newly emerging nation-state that did its best to curtail the montonera's activities, with little success. So powerful were the Pincheiras that it took the Chilean state more than a decade to capture them. The Pincheiras' political activities against the Chilean state not only predisposed the state's reactions to them but also played a role in the state's policies for the country beginning a year after Pincheira's capture. "The extinction of those bands contributed significantly in securing peace and confidence in the southern provinces. It was of invaluable benefit for industrial progress. *It should also strengthen the prestige and power of the government.*"[59] The result was a more restrictive and conservative constitution, with specific measures to prevent new Pincheiras from arising in the future.

Banditry returned in the middle of the nineteenth century, but as some historians have argued, it was more a response to the changing socioeconomic conditions and evolving cultural practices of the countryside than a phenomenon that had national ramifications. Analyses of this banditry have focused on relationships between elites and peasants on a localized level that did not necessarily effect a national response on the part of the state, even though Chilean authorities often attempted to "legislate on questions of subaltern morality and sociability."[60] Because a "criminal code was not introduced in Chile until the 1870s, such legislation was often enacted for much of the century at a regional level through the edicts of provincial authorities."[61]

In his *Historia Jeneral de Chile*, Diego Barros Arana argued that the "Araucanian frontier, that is the Bío-Bío line, had been pacified since 1827."[62] He attributed this "pacification" to the resignation in the mid-1820s of some Mapuches who had originally supported Pico, Hermosilla, and Sinosiain. Those who followed Pincheira and did not surrender to the state were still a problem. Considering the state's push toward the conquest and acquisition of Araucanía, its triumph over the Pincheira brothers becomes even more significant. Not only did the Pincheiras represent a threat to state stability, but they also jeopardized state expansion. Although José Antonio's capture and the final dissolution of the montonera did not end the struggles in Araucanía, they did strengthen the state's determination to eventually conquer the Mapuche and subjugate them to mainstream Chilean society, a process that took the rest of the century to complete and is discussed in chapter 6.

Conclusion

Throughout the decade of the 1820s, Chile's leaders spent a great deal of time attempting to disband the Pincheira brothers' montonera, with little success. The Pincheiras' network of spies, links to the various communities in Araucanía, and alliance with the Pehuenches made them a powerful force that threatened the process of nation building in the new republic. They also impeded the state's plans for further expansion into Araucanía and the subjugation of the Mapuche. This chapter has analyzed the Pincheira brothers' montonera, exploring their relationships with the local community and the possible motivations for their successful twelve-year "career" against the Chilean state, the state's eventual regrouping, the capture of José Antonio Pincheira, and disbandment of the montonera. The montonera's dissolution allowed the state to consolidate its power base and strengthen the process of state formation in the country. The Pincheira brothers allied with the Pehuenches, a subgroup of the Mapuche. During the tumultuous period of independence, the Pincheiras' alliance, along with other Mapuche partnerships, impeded the development of the Chilean state, as this chapter has illustrated. Nonetheless, Mapuche alliances also served to illustrate the changing nature of Mapuche politics and economics, a subject discussed in the next chapter.

CHAPTER FOUR

Mapuche Alliances

CHILE'S INDEPENDENCE IN 1818 and the subsequent political chaos of the 1820s formed a backdrop for the dramatic changes taking place within the Mapuche communities of Araucanía. The newly formed state's southern expansion and settlement of indigenous lands began with its systematic destruction of an already deeply fragmented society. The Chilean state ended the remaining Spanish threat in the south during the early years of the 1820s by exacerbating existing fracture lines among indigenous groups, and it later worked to undermine indigenous resistance by forming alliances with friendly Mapuches.

This chapter discusses the complicated relationship between different Mapuche divisions and Chile's newly formed state during the early decades of the nineteenth century, with specific emphasis on the Pehuenche division from Chillán and their enemies (including the Pehuenches of Trapatrapa). The Chilean state's continual push southward encroached upon Mapuche lands and Mapuche autonomy from state authority, and while some divisions decided to cooperate with the state, the Chillán Pehuenches and their allies did not. Instead, they fought a guerrilla war against the state for twelve years, during which they successfully thwarted state attempts to take possession of their lands and their control of commerce in the region. Throughout this period, these Pehuenches sustained their autonomy in their territory and in their commercial relations, and forced the state to adopt more restrictive national measures against them. Furthermore, since the state's goals of conquest and settlement required state control of Araucanía, the Pehuenches' efforts effectively delayed both conquest and settlement until later in the century.

Although it is difficult to decipher Mapuche motivations from Spanish and Chilean sources, evidence presented in this chapter supports the notion that Mapuches were not passive participants in first an imperial and then a national objective of conquest and subjugation to the dominant European Chilean society. Rather, it was the newly created Chilean state's strategy to manipulate already contentious indigenous politics among different Mapuche groups, while simultaneously using indigenous practices, that resulted in Mapuche submission by the latter third of the nineteenth century.

Colonial Background

During the colonial period, religion and trade played a significant role between different Mapuche groups and their relationships with the Spanish crown. The Spanish erected forts to defend against Mapuche attacks and sent missionaries into Araucanía to convert the "barbarous" Mapuches to Christianity, an approach carried out under the guidance of Father Pedro de Valdivia and his fellow priests of the Society of Jesus.[1] Valdivia's plan, known as *la guerra defensiva* (the defensive war, 1612–1626), called for voluntary Christianization, to be accomplished through the work of missionaries sent to Mapuche communities that asked for them, and an end to *encomienda* labor and Indian slavery. In return, Mapuches worked on a tribute basis for *encomenderos* (colonists granted people to work for them), and hacendados communicated any maritime activity on the Araucanian coast to Spanish officials, returned any Christian captives to the colonial state, and did not cross the frontier line, except for royal officials traveling to Chiloé Island. Valdivia's vision differed from previous attempts at conquest in the region because he embraced Mapuche cultural differences without debasing or minimizing their importance, while at the same time working toward a colonization scheme that included the Spanish goal of Christianization on Mapuche terms. What followed were long periods of peace interspersed with periodic Mapuche uprisings—in 1655, 1723, and 1766.[2]

The primary tool that both sides utilized to maintain peace was the parlamento, or peace negotiation. These ceremonies were formal in nature, with elaborate rituals that included specific food, drink, and dress. Parlamentos usually lasted several days, and thousands of people attended them. The Spanish crown and later the newly established Chilean state sent high-ranking officials to these gatherings, a testament to the importance of the peace accords produced at parlamentos. On the Mapuche side, depending on which group or groups were in negotiations, the usual practice was to have various caciques with their accompanying retinues of *mocetones* (warriors) and *lenguaraces* (translators), often numbering in the hundreds. A significant aspect of a parlamento meeting involved specific speech patterns and the exchange of gifts. During the colonial period, parlamentos acted as control mechanisms, allowing the Spanish crown to colonize and evangelize Mapuches (albeit minimally and not very successfully) and allowing Mapuches to maintain their autonomy and independence against Spanish colonial policies. After independence, parlamentos continued to be conducted within a radically altered landscape that proved much less tenable for Mapuches and more advantageous for the new Chilean Republic, a subject discussed in detail in the next chapter.

Despite the crown's attempts at religious conversion, conflicts between different Mapuche groups and the Spanish crown continued throughout the colonial period and caused dramatic changes within Machupe political structure. Prior to Spanish incursions on their lands, Mapuches maintained a fairly decentralized political structure, whereby family units played a dominant role. Continual resistance against the Spanish, however, increased the importance of war leaders and decreased the importance of family members. By the beginning of the nineteenth century, political power rested within a hierarchy of about one hundred caciques named *loncos*.[3] Each lonco governed within specific geographical boundaries, and their power was not necessarily based on their merits. Political centralization also necessitated a change in how Mapuche loncos distributed power among themselves, since they now held these posts permanently. A hierarchy developed, with fifteen to twenty *ñidol loncos*, "the grand men," at the top. Then came loncos, followed by regional caciques and then caciques, all of whom were subordinate to one of the ñidol loncos. Family members often made up the hierarchy, with the children of important loncos and regional caciques inheriting political power from their fathers. Good leadership continued to consist of wisdom, oral skills, and war techniques, which all cacique children learned: "[The son of the cacique] received a special education. He was taught to ride a horse from a young age. . . . He knew how to use the lance and he underwent a period of training under the tutelage of a captain to learn the art of war."[4] Despite changes in the political system, Mapuche divisions (Llanos, Arribanos, Abajinos, Pehuenches, and so on) were not necessarily united under one political banner. Throughout the colonial period and early nineteenth century, ñidol loncos periodically seized power over lesser caciques, often leading to warfare and the domination of one division over another.

The Pehuenches

The Pehuenches were a Mapuche division that lived in the central-south region of the Andes cordillera in Araucanía. This was an area characterized by extraordinarily high peaks, ravines, lakes, and forests. Their strategic geographic location enabled the Pehuenches to manage a lucrative trade network in which they maintained considerable influence over other Mapuche groups on both sides of the Andes cordillera.[5]

The Pehuenche trade network within the colonial economy included cattle ranching and rustling, salt mining, the capture of guanacos (a cousin of the llama) and ostriches, and subsistence farming. Of these sources of income, salt was the most important for trade, and there were two different kinds: "The first . . . is more fine, but more difficult to collect and less abundant. . . . The sodium chloride prevalent in Pehuenche territory is very pure, at times of a light pink color and it deserves to be preferred over the other dirty type that is obtained by Chileans near the mouth of the Maule [River]."[6] The Pehuenches controlled salt production and distribution among the various Mapuche divisions, who used salt as a preservative for the meat products each group traded. So important was salt that "the most revered gift that one could give in the furthest villages from the frontier were a few pounds of rock salt."[7] The Pehuenches provided much-needed salt and guidance across mountainous Andean terrain into territory on the eastern side of the cordillera in exchange for goods, including cattle and horses.[8]

Colonial trade also benefitted Spanish settlers on the frontier. It became increasingly important throughout the seventeenth and eighteenth centuries as the trade network itself evolved from one that was subsistence based to a full-scale commercial economy. Mapuches and especially Pehuenches were the dominant players in this market.[9] Furthermore, the gradual change from subsistence trade to outright commercial activities for profit and personal wealth influenced Mapuches' relationships with Spanish-creole settlers in Araucanía. There essentially existed two types of relationships that often overlapped, "that of the Mapuche with the Spanish-Creole military and that of the Mapuche with merchants."[10] Conchavadores, who were either Spanish-creoles or mestizos, acted as economic intermediaries between the Spanish colonial state and the different Mapuche groups in Araucanía.

From the sixteenth through the middle of the eighteenth century, Pehuenches posed a threat to Spanish-creoles only sporadically when they, allied with other Mapuche groups, attacked the forts in the region of the Maule, Ñuble, Itata, and Laja Rivers. Increased trade between the Pehuenches and the Spanish-creoles by the end of the eighteenth century, however, convinced Spanish-creole authorities that an alliance with them would be useful in defending areas east of the rivers. Likewise, the Pehuenches needed the help of Spanish-creoles in their battles against their enemies, the Huilliches (another Mapuche division), who had a considerable hold on the pampas. The Huilliches fought against the Pehuenches for natural resources on the western side of the Andes.

After independence, the newly formed Chilean state sought to extend its territorial boundary southward. In independent Chile, these commercial relationships at first enabled the Mapuche to defend and to maintain their autonomy from state encroachment. For example, in 1819 Andrés Alcázar, commander of the frontier, wrote to his superior in Concepción, Ramón Freire, to tell him that he was waiting for a Pehuenche cacique named Cabuagüe and forty of his mocetones and that they were coming for the business of salt and some horses.[11] These particular Pehuenches were not necessarily allied to the newly independent state but were willing to trade with it, illustrating the increasing interdependence and importance of trade across ethnic lines in Araucanía. State officials preserved important food supplies for the army with the salt, and the Pehuenches utilized the horses for their various malones against other Mapuche groups as well as against the Chilean state.

After independence, the newly formed Chilean state also utilized parlamentos in its push southward. However, as we will see later in this chapter and the next, Mapuches continued to dominate the parlamento system, at least until 1825, and the Chilean state had to hammer out agreements with Mapuches under indigenous rules. After the constitution of 1833, it became increasingly difficult for Mapuches to defend their territory and maintain their autonomy, as the newly consolidated Chilean state gathered its considerable resources to enforce what it considered to be its southern territorial boundary. It also formed alliances with "friendly" Mapuche groups, such as the Abajinos, whose main caciques during this period were Colipí and Coñoepán, and the Trapatrapa Pehuenches of the south. Others, such as the Arribanos, led by Mariluán, and the Pehuenches of Chillán, formed alliances against the Chilean government.[12] Nonetheless, as this chapter and the next demonstrate, even these alliances were tenuous at best.

For the Chillán Pehuenches, the guerrilla warfare in the south was an opportunity to assert power over other Mapuche divisions in their region and maintain their autonomy in trade relations. All Pehuenches traded with other Mapuches as well as Chileans. However, they also fought among themselves.[13] Sometime in the early 1820s, the Chillán Pehuenches officially joined the royalist Pincheira brothers' montonera that was allied with the holdout Spanish army near Concepción. These Pehuenches joined the Pincheiras because they believed the Spanish crown had respected their political and economic autonomy throughout the colonial period. Furthermore, these Pehuenches did not trust Chile, a newly formed state they did not recognize. "For [them], there was a considerable difference between the Spanish and the Chileans and they feared a central government from Santiago, who with armed forces, could attack and overtake their territory."[14]

From 1819 to 1822, the Pehuenche–Pincheira montonera fought as part of Vicente Benavides's army. After his death in 1822, it continued under General Juan Manuel Pico's command. Pico's death in 1824 severely weakened the Spanish army in the south and it stopped supplying the Pehuenche–Pincheira montonera with munitions, men, and a reason for fighting. No longer under anyone's command, the montonera took on a different character and purpose, but it stayed together until the Chilean army captured the montonera's leader, José Antonio Pincheira, eight years later. (See chapter 3.)

Between 1819 and 1824, Mapuches fought each other as traditional enemies, only this time their rivalries were tied to their allegiances either to the remaining Spanish officers or to the Chilean state. Those Mapuches who allied with the state took the opportunity to "ask for soldiers to accompany them into enemy territory and conduct bloody malones against their rivals."[15] The Battle of Gualeguayco of November 1822, between Captain Manuel Bulnes and Juan Manuel Pico, exemplifies the animosity between the different Mapuche groups. Captain Bulnes allied with five hundred friendly Mapuches under the command of the caciques Venancio Coihuepán and Lorenzo Peñoleo. Pico and his faithful ally, the cacique Francisco Mariluán, who was also the fierce enemy of Coihuepán and Peñoleo, led a cavalry of eight hundred. In the end, Pico's army was no match for Bulnes, who won the battle. Pico lost eighty men while Bulnes lost only twelve.[16] Nonetheless, Pico and Mariluán continued fighting until Pico's death in October 1824, although Mariluán made an overture for peace earlier that year. In fact, as one historian asserts, Pico continued fighting only because of his alliances with the Mapuches, and especially with Mariluán and another cacique named Maguil.[17] The inclusion of the Pincheira brothers' montonera and their Pehuenche allies after Vicente Benavides's death in February 1822 aided in nominally prolonging the royalist cause on the southern frontier until 1824.

The Battle of Gualeguayco also illustrates how the emergent Chilean state took advantage of already existing frictions between Mapuche groups to further its own agenda of territorial expansion and indigenous subjugation in Araucanía. In fact, it is precisely the defense of their trade network that compelled the Pehuenches of the Chillán area to join the Pincheiras' montonera. Power conflicts between the leaders of the different Pehuenche groups over who controlled the trade networks compelled one group to side with the state and the other to join the Pincheiras' montonera.

In the end, protecting territory and maintaining control of a profitable trade network proved more important to the Pehuenche–Pincheira montonera than even royalist ideology. For the Pehuenches of Chillán, and by extension any Mapuche groups that did not support the Chilean state, these goals were especially important, since their struggles with the Chilean state did not end with the dissolution of the Pehuenche–Pincheira montonera in 1832. The Pincheira–Pehuenche montonera also conducted malones all over Araucanía and as far east as Mendoza. For example, in 1824 the montonera attacked the outlying areas of Niquén, in the cordillera. After looting the town, the montonera "locked fourteen old women in the chapel and set it ablaze along with the rest of the houses in the town."[18] Soon after they left, taking all the young women of the village with them. These activities became so commonplace that "the bandits considered themselves owners of the area, in such a manner that if a judge was named to give an order [to pursue them], within days he was found assassinated, a signal of the bandits' complete authority."[19]

The montonera's malones were not restricted to towns and cities. On one occasion, "in February 1828, in less than half an hour, they sacked the houses of the Talcarehue hacienda, without pardoning the inquilinos' plots of lands, committing several murders, and taking with them 2,000 head of cattle."[20] The Pehuenches and Pincheiras' men took many of the women as concubines and wives and traded the cattle within their commercial network, which included other allied Mapuche groups from both sides of the cordillera.[21] The Chilean state saw these activities as criminal. The Pehuenches and their bandit allies, however, may have seen these activities as an assertion of authority in a region over which they held economic and political control.

The Pincheiras' alliances with Mapuches throughout the early 1820s were key to their success. Several Mapuche caciques, including Francisco Mariluán, leader of the Arribanos, or Llanistas as they are sometimes called, cooperated with the Pincheiras.[22] Historian Benjamín Vicuña Mackenna describes Mariluán as a "small, but muscular man with a tanned body and face. . . . He was a very brave Indian, a fighter, who threw himself from his horse in the middle of a battle and fought on foot with only his lance, to encourage his men to fight."[23] Additionally, Vicuña Mackenna attributes to Mariluán a degree of rationality he did not concede to other caciques. As a child Mariluán was educated at the mission school Colegio de Propaganda Fide de Chillán.[24] There he learned Spanish, which he spoke fluently, and learned certain notions about government and religion.[25] Two of his sons also studied at the Colegio de Propaganda Fide,[26] the same school where many Pehuenche caciques from the Chillán area who later joined the Pincheira brothers' montonera were educated. Mariulán is an example of an indigenous leader who, through his early education, encountered Spanish values, and his cooperation with the royalist Pincheiras can be understood in this context.

Mariluán's loyalty to Juan Manuel Pico originated from his education at the Colegio de Propaganda Fide.[27] In 1779 the Spanish government began paying Mariluán a salary as a "cacique governor of Bureo," and he attended many parlamentos as a Spanish official.[28] His distrust of the new government in Santiago after independence was the outcome of his—and by extension the Arribanos'—fear that the new state would take away the land and autonomy that the Spanish crown had ceded to them through previous parlamentos. After more than a century of parlamentos and peace with the Spanish, "who never intended to take their lands,"[29] Mariluán's fears were not without merit.

Mariluán provided Pico with men, arms, and shelter in his lands located in Collico.[30] For example, at the Battle of Gualeguayco, many of the eight hundred men on horseback were Mariluán's warriors. Yet for all his reputed loyalty to Juan Manuel Pico, and subsequently to the Spanish crown, Mariluán began to show signs of a possible about-face in January 1824, ten months before Pico's death. In a January 6 letter to Pedro Barnachea, Mariluán expressed his desires for a peace settlement and discussed his recruitment of neighboring caciques who were willing to participate in such a forum:

> Everything here has been good and now we are only waiting for you to send us [Captain] Ortiz so he may go with the ambassadors that should be going from all the *reducciones* [indigenous communities], and also those from the coast who I am currently waiting for and if they do not go, those from this butralmapu will go in order to not delay our work; do not listen to any stories saying otherwise . . . and because I am a man, I know well that I have given you my word and I know how to carry it out.[31]

In a previous letter dated two days earlier, Mariluán had detailed several conversations between his brother Cachulef and various caciques who decided to participate in the peace negotiations. He claimed that Cachulef had "all the reducciones of Caillín under his command and he had succeeded in stopping any further malocas against the Spanish and other Indians."[32]

A peace junta took place between the different caciques, as *lenguarás* (Indian translator) Rafael Burgos described in a letter to Pedro Barnachea:

> A grand junta has taken place, attended by caciques from all the

reducciones from Malleco to the Bío-Bío, and it has ended very favorably. The head of the junta was cacique Cauchuli who helped me and he spoke very forcefully. . . . I am writing to let you know how much work I have done to have some agreements, although Marilúan was a bit jealous of what was accomplished. . . . Yesterday we had another junta and it was also a success. Mariluán sent General Miguel Salazar after the Pehuenches of Loles and Lonquimai. The situation there is very disorganized because of a maloca from Melipan that killed many people, among them a cacique Gicilipan and his son. They have also taken many families captive.[33]

The junta discussed the political situation among the different Mapuche groups, and it appeared that Cacique Melipan was not cooperating with the rest of the caciques, preferring instead to raid a nearby Pehuenche cacique's territory, killing him and his son and taking many captives. Mariluán, aware that the situation with Melipan posed a threat to his ongoing discussions with the Chilean state, sent emissaries to attempt to dissuade Melipan from any further violence.

The state, however, had reason to believe that some foul play was taking place. On January 3, 1824, an officer of the state sent a notice to General Juan de Dios Rivera, at the time intendant of Concepción:

Facundo Bravo has just arrived. He claims he left Mariluán on Sunday the 28th of the past month [December 1823] in the afternoon to go to his house, from which he left Monday for here. He claims it was for the sole purpose of visiting his family. Without a doubt, he is either a spy of Pico or of Mariluán because Burgos' mail left from the same place also on the 28th in the afternoon when Pico was already meeting with Mariluán as we mentioned to you in dispatch N. 130 dated December 31, 1823. He says that Pico neither sees nor hears Mariluán, and all he knows is that the Indians were on their way to conduct a maloca in Lumaco but that Mariluán was not participating; on the contrary, per what Burgos tells me and consequently it is being sent to you in bad faith.[34]

In March, Mariluán wrote a response to Barnachea in which he refuted the accusation that he was still allied with Pico and aiding him. He said he had not spoken with Pico for several days and that his people were providing aid to the Pehuenche cacique, Collipal, because Melipan had attacked him due to the hold that Melipan had in that region. He lamented that he had "prevented malones from occurring . . . and if this fire starts [the one between Melipan and the Pehuenches], it will be useless trying to put it out. And I will say this, that my job will have been for naught after having completed it to the best of my abilities. Furthermore, he "was sending ambassadors with his brother Cachulef" to prove that he had done his job in good faith.[35]

Mariluán intended to hold a forum within the Mapuche community to establish peace in the region, and many caciques seemed willing to discuss peace, except for the Pehuenches of Trapatrapa, whose reluctance made Mariluán's overtures to the state less secure. The state was not convinced, however, as Juan de Dios Rivera explained in a letter to Pedro Barnachea: "Burgos has returned with the caciques from the conference. The conference with them has been reduced to what we have witnessed so many times already."[36] At that conference the different Mapuche groups agreed only to return families within fifteen days and that two of their caciques would meet in Yumbel.[37]

In response, Mariluán severed his relationship with Manuel Pico and then informed General Manuel Bulnes of Pico's whereabouts: "Mariluán has given us notice in his letter, which I include with this dispatch, that Pico has been reunited with Pincheira; they have arrived from Llamaico where they had gone to conduct malones and that very soon they will go to Chillán accompanied by their Pehuenche allies."[38]

By May 1824 military personnel became convinced that "Mariluán's behavior deserve[d] the consideration of the government."[39] Nonetheless, some royalist factions attempted to deter Mariluán from surrendering: "Burgos tells me that cacique Yanpi of the coast and ten of his warriors have called upon Mariluán to tell him that under no circumstances should he surrender to the *patria* (fatherland) and that a ship has arrived on the coast and is waiting to take him away."[40]

Two months later, in July, "Mariluán arrived with caciques Carril and Meliquin to tell Pico not to continue because if they were found out he [Mariluán] would look bad in the eyes of the government of the *patria*. He asked them to return to their own lands to continue their malón at another time."[41] Pico refused and continued his march toward San Carlos, recruiting

Mapuches from Collico, Quecheraguas, Bureo, and Purrín. In San Carlos, he combined his forces with those of the Pehuenche–Pincheira montonera, with the intent to conduct malones in the surrounding areas.[42] Significantly, Mariluán, because of his ongoing negotiations with the Chilean state, did not participate personally in any of Pico's malones, despite the active involvement of some of his own people.[43]

The continued allegiance to Pico of some of Mariluán's people attests to the complicated nature of Mapuche politics during this period. Within the Mapuche political system, Mariluán was a lonco, with power over other regional caciques under him, such as his brother Cachulef. As powerful as he was, however, Mariluán's political authority was not universal. And since he did ally with Pico for a lengthy period, his switching sides alarmed some of his people who believed otherwise, and therefore they continued to support Pico. His failure to convince some of the lesser caciques, such as Melipan, to surrender with him indicates the limits of his political authority within the larger hierarchical Mapuche political system.

Mariluán's limited political authority was an indication of the general distrust Mapuches had of political power, even with the changes that came about in their political system. A system that went from decentralized political power, where family units played a major role and caciques were chosen upon their merits and only for short intervals, to a centralized hierarchical political system with inherited political power had its limits, in that political power did not always rest on one individual. Thus we have within Mapuche society what sociologist Pierre Clastres has called "a society against the state."[44] For Clastres, society defines political power. If chiefly authority collapses, then leaders fail to achieve their goals.[45]

After Pico's death in October 1824, Mariluán sent a message to Pincheira announcing it, but Pincheira did not believe him and decided to visit Mariluán to "learn the truth."[46] Whether Pincheira learned the truth or not is not clear, but "Barnachea finally succeeded with his plan of peace and convinced Mariluán to attend a parlamento, held in Tapihue in January 1825, where Mariluán accepted the terms of peace and the system of government, while Barnachea recognized the Araucanians [Mapuches] as having the same rights as those of Chileans."[47]

Peace lasted only a few months because, as the state describes it, "within the same year Mariluán joined Pincheira and terror and vandalism once again took over the countryside, principally in the areas between Bureo and la Laja."[48] For two years Mariluán remained allied to the Pincheira brothers, aiding them whenever the occasion demanded it.[49] Once again, the state had to reorganize its efforts against its enemies to ensure peace and stability in Araucanía, a process not completed until the spring and summer[50] of 1826–1827, when General Beauchef's three-pronged expedition conducted a new military campaign in the south. Although the expedition itself failed to catch the Pehuenche–Pincheira montonera, it succeeded in reining in Mariluán, who surrendered to the state in the fall of 1827.

One of the most powerful caciques during this period, Mariluán surrendered twice, once in 1825 and again in 1827. Most of the Mapuche divisions with whom Mariluán had previously been in contact also surrendered in 1827, but the Pincheiras and their Pehuenche followers did not. Unlike Mariluán, the Pehuenches who followed the Pincheira brothers were not willing to surrender anything to the state, even when Pincheira himself worked out a plan of action for his final surrender. As seen previously, during the first set of negotiations for peace with Mariluán in 1824, these Pehuenches repeatedly rejected any gestures of peace and attempted to convince Mariluán to ally with them instead. Mariluán, however, refused to join them. The Pehuenches of Trapatrapa (region south of Chillán) sent two mocetones and a cacique to ask Mariluán for aid in helping them maloquear around. They also complained to him that the division from this plaza had made them march and had taken many of them captive. Mariluán responded that "he did not want to fight . . . and that they . . . should defend themselves as they choose but that he would not mount a horse."[51]

The Pehuenches of Trapatrapa, like those who followed the Pincheira brothers, too had a powerful hold on trade in the region. For example, in 1824 they "assassinated eight merchants who had minutes before entered the plaza with their goods . . . they stole more than one-hundred animals."[52] However, the same dispatch reveals that an army division was in the area just before the merchants arrived, [53] perhaps threatening the Pehuenches' control of trade in their lands. These Pehuenches had earlier accused the state of "selling their land and that it has been impossible for any merchant to conduct trade because they have their goods taken away from them."[54] The state's tactics of pitting one Mapuche group against another worked well in the case of Mariluán and the Pehuenches of Trapatrapa. Even though these

Pehuenches did not want to surrender with Mariluán, they made it clear that the reason for not doing so was the state's repeated attempts to disrupt their hold on trade and their relationships with other Mapuche divisions, especially Mariluán's group. Thus these Pehuenches (mortal enemies of the Pehuenches who followed the Pincheira brothers) were now working on the same side. As an example, in the summer of 1826–1827, when General Beauchef's expedition set out against the Pincheiras, the Trapatrapa Pehuenches found themselves in a difficult position. General Beauchef asked them for guidance across rough mountainous terrain, which they provided but with no guarantees of any further cooperation.

Mariluán's final surrender in 1827 signaled more economic problems for the Trapatrapa Pehuenches. Now that Mariluán was allied with the state, trade within his lands was effectively blocked, restricting the power these Pehuenches held over commercial dealings in this region. In contrast, allying with the Pincheira brothers and their former enemies, the Chillán Pehuenches, enabled the Trapatrapa Pehuenches to continue their activities in direct defiance of established state authority.

The alliance worked until José Antonio Pincheira surrendered to the state in 1832. The Pehuenches returned to their lands in the cordillera, where they continued to trade with Mapuche divisions on both sides of the cordillera, although they strengthened their relationship with the Mapuches on the eastern side. With increased pressure from the Chilean state to gain access to and eventual ownership of Mapuche lands in Araucanía, including those of the Pehuenches, "an Araucanian diaspora [began] from the cordillera, in part pushed by this pressure on their lands, but also pulled by the riches to be found in the Argentine desert."[55] As the century progressed, and Chilean agriculture continued to expand south and east, the Chileans "moved to claim all 'surplus' lands not legally recognized as Indian lands . . . earlier."[56] By 1858 the first German colonists had arrived in the south to cultivate untilled lands.[57] For those Mapuches who remained in Araucanía, their options were limited to either working with the state or war.[58] The Pehuenches found themselves isolated in the cordillera, with little support from either the Chilean state or other Mapuche groups.

Conclusion

Using the case of the Pehuenches of Chillán and their enemies, the Trapa-trapa Pehuenches, and Mariluán and the Arribanos, this chapter chartered the complicated and confusing terrain of interethnic political rivalries between different Mapuche groups and the Chilean state after independence. Centralization of Mapuche political structures, coupled with continuing geographical and economic conflicts within different Mapuche subgroups, allowed the Chilean state to form alliances that took advantage of internal conflicts and to advance its agenda of southern territorial expansion in Araucanía. Nonetheless, groups such as the Chillán Pehuenches, along with their bandit allies, as well as other Mapuches, continued to militarily resist state encroachment on their lands and negotiated varying degrees of autonomy at parlamentos throughout the better part of the nineteenth century, a subject discussed at length in the next chapter.

CHAPTER FIVE

Parlamentos

ON JANUARY 7, 1825, MARILUÁN AND THE FOURTEEN *BUTRAMALPUS* (indigenous territorial divisions) that he represented sat down with Pedro Barnachea, commander of the army of the frontier, and hammered out an agreement known as the Parlamento of Tapihue. Although this was the first parlamento between the Chilean Republic (after Chilean independence) and the Mapuche,[1] it was not named a parlamento but rather a series of *tratados* (treaties).[2] This chapter analyzes the changing nature of the parlamento, a formal dialogue between Mapuches and representatives of the Spanish crown or Chilean Republic, from the middle of the eighteenth century until the middle of the nineteenth century. In taking a closer look at the Parlamento of Negrete in 1726, the Parlamento of Tapihue in 1774, and the parlamentos of 1803, 1814, 1825, 1860, and 1871, I reveal a sharp contrast between eighteenth-century parlamentos and their nineteenth-century counterparts. Specifically, the agreements made between various Mapuche groups and representatives of the Spanish crown at multiday celebrations in the eighteenth century followed patterns and rituals that were markedly absent in both Tapihue in 1825 and subsequent parlamentos. The question remains, however: What, if anything, did the parlamentos achieve? What were each side's goals? Did these goals change between parlamentos like Tapihue at the close of the eighteenth century and those in the nineteenth century, especially after independence and the creation of the Chilean nation-state? In this chapter, I consider how the Tapihue Tratado of 1825 was different from the others (see appendix) conducted between the Mapuches and the Spanish crown since the first one celebrated in Quillín in 1641, speculating on its new meaning in the post-independence era. I also observe new trends in the structure and rituals of parlamentos celebrated after 1825. A neglected but important feature of the parlamentos was how significant they were to their Mapuche participants. Were these parlamentos a tool for maintaining Mapuche independence from the Spanish? If so, when and how did the meaning of these dialogues change under the Chilean Republic?

Since the two negotiating parties at the table were no longer the same, the parlamentos necessarily changed from the end of the eighteenth century to the early nineteenth century. After independence, the different Mapuche groups, who were less united than during the colonial period, had to contend with a unified nation-state in the form of the Chilean Republic. The contents of the parlamentos themselves also evolved, placing the Mapuches at a disadvantage even though they were being promised full citizenship within the *familia chilena* in the newly formed Chilean Republic. As this chapter argues, nation and citizenship meant something very different to both sides negotiating at these parlamentos, and the Chilean view won out. The repercussions after 1825 effectively destroyed Mapuche independence and autonomy and required that they capitulate to state demands, becoming second-class citizens within their own lands.

The first parlamento took place on January 6, 1641, near the midway point between the Quillem and Choll-Choll Rivers. Known as the Parlamento of Quillín, this peace accord sought to draw the border between Spanish and Mapuche territory, which was determined to lie at the Bío-Bío in the north and the Toltén in the south. The region between these two rivers became known as Araucanía and was considered independent Mapuche territory. Additionally, Spaniards agreed to evacuate from Angol, although the fort of Arauco remained under Spanish control. The Mapuches agreed to leave missionaries to do their work, return prisoners, and not cause trouble or go beyond the frontier line.[3] Most significantly, this parlamento guaranteed the Mapuche complete independence within the frontier borders of the Bío-Bío and the Toltén Rivers. In other words, Mapuches were not a part of the Captaincy of Chile and therefore were considered a separate state, "a condition [that] was not a 'gracious concession' of his majesty, and it cost approximately 5.5 million Mapuche casualties."[4] While this first parlamento appeared to broker peace between the Europeans and indigenous peoples, its effect was incomplete.

Parlamentos did not halt the ubiquitous violence present in the region, whether it was Spanish parties that crossed the Bío-Bío to capture Mapuches and sell them as slaves in Santiago or encomenderos further north,[5] or Mapuches who crossed the boundary line to conduct malones against hacendados and ranchers. Indeed, the endemic violence in Araucanía has spurred some debate as to what exactly parlamentos achieved during this period. The Estudios Fronterizos School maintains that, for the most part, parlamentos were a tool to control and derail criminals, known as *afuerinos*, in frontier society. The afuerinos were men who "fought to be seen as free men, but Spanish Creoles and Mapuches treated them as deserters and renegades."[6] The afuerino was much like the "llaneros of the Apure and the gauchos of the Pampas, . . . with crude physical features, who was feared not only because he was an outsider, but because in his face one could read the history of a subject created outside of the system."[7] Afuerinos also took advantage of the fragile peace in Araucanía to involve themselves in illegal trade and other forms of criminality. Thus, in many ways, afuerinos resembled nineteenth-century bandits.[8] They were outside the law, and both afuerinos and bandits preyed on and traded with Mapuches and Europeans. They were effectively borderlands people, not fully part of either Mapuche or creole society. Parlamentos, then, acted as peace negotiations that effectively blocked afuerinos' possible criminal activities.

Other scholars, such as Guillame Boccara, Antonio Varas, and Fernando Casanueva, disagree with the Estudios Fronterizos School, claiming that the parlamento was a colonial tool to subordinate Mapuches to creole society under the Spanish crown. Guillame Boccara argues that the Spanish authorities used parlamentos to control the Mapuche and to get them to become more civilized—that is, part of Spanish society: "Those two institutions [parlamentos and missions] had as their goal to supervise and 'civilize' the Indians via the inculcation of the 'true culture and religion' as well as the implementation of common legal norms. But, aside from this multifaceted politics of normalization, Mapuches continued cultivating their specificity, obeying their own cultural guidelines and watching their own territorial independence."[9]

Fernando Casanueva claims that in the colonial period, warfare and legal enslavement made Mapuche resistance more ferocious. For him, "the geo-political reality imposed on the Crown was to carry out 'parlamentos of peace' periodically with the 'rebellious' Indians (whom they designated ambassadors in Santiago), thus recognizing their freedom; however, without ever renouncing their projects of submission."[10] Casanueva argues that the crown never deviated from imposing notions of a civilized society on the Indians, "for a man in colonial society (hacendado, campesino, administrator, clergyman, chronicler, merchant, etc.) the world, his civilized world, creole, mestizo and Christian, reached until the Bío-Bío River, even farther until Chiloé were the lands of the 'barbarians,' rebellious Indians, kingless, lawless, faithless, constituting a permanent threat, real or imaginary, for the Kingdom, with whom it maintained warlike and peaceful contacts (commerce, barter, missions, parlamentos)."[11] These parlamentos, in addition to subjugating Mapuches to colonial Spanish society, also deterred criminal elements by setting both physical and political boundaries between the different Mapuche groups and the Spanish crown.

What becomes clear throughout the analysis of the parlamentos in the eighteenth century and prior to independence is that Mapuches, whether afuerinos or ferocious defenders of their lands, maintained independence over their territory (Araucanía). Furthermore, Mapuches utilized the parlamento structure to make explicit demands of the Spanish crown that strengthened their territorial and political independence. Beginning with Tapihue in 1825, that same parlamento mechanism served the interests of the Chilean state because Araucanía was now part of the geographical boundaries of the state. Therefore Mapuches themselves were now subject to state law and state authority.

Parlamentos in the Eighteenth Century

In the eighteenth century, parlamentos had a slightly different character. In addition to negotiating peace, the Spanish and Mapuches used parlamentos as a tool to police and mitigate the violence in Araucanía; parlamentos during this period were "done in an environment that was more conducive to peace than war . . . [they were] cordial yet formal."[12] Also, parlamentos became huge, grand, multiday affairs with hundreds and sometimes thousands in attendance, and the Spanish spared no expense in providing the most costly food and drink available at the time, particularly wheat, meat, wine, and aguardiente. Fresh beef was a favorite of Mapuche attendees.[13] The most important alcoholic beverage was wine, and Spaniards spent thousands of pesos on the most expensive wines available, which conchavadores traded in large quantities in Araucanía. Wine had several uses in the eighteenth-century parlamentos, including as ceremonial objects. For example, a large bonfire was extinguished with wine at the 1771 Parlamento of Negrete.[14] The wine brought by Spanish authorities also guaranteed a large audience of indigenous caciques and others, because Mapuches "felt a particular attraction to this beverage and esteemed it highly."[15]

Eighteenth-century parlamentos had a more festive atmosphere than the peace treaty parlamentos of the earlier period. According to one historian, parlamentos during this period were "a motive to party, of a celebration between Indians and Creoles; [they] permitted peoples of different customs and different tastes to eat and drink well. [They] were an expression of official hispanoindigenous relations."[16] The celebratory components of these parlamentos cost the Spanish crown thousands of pesos that often had to be cobbled together through various sources intended for other crown interests in the region.[17]

Additionally, multiday parlamentos followed certain rituals and procedures. It was customary, for example, to have pre-parlamento talks, usually called juntas.[18] At the actual parlamento, Mapuche caciques from the different groups in attendance often stated their case at specific intervals. Both parties present tended to assume certain behaviors: "They treat with each other [Mapuches and the Spanish] in good faith, because they [Mapuches] see it entrenched in the Royal word and in the oath of religion, that they well know that the Spanish see these as sacrosanct and their infraction as criminal."[19] Although Mapuches were "barbarous" and a "vanquished enemy," they were nonetheless sensitive to the customs kept at these negotiations. Therefore, it was imperative for the Spanish to maintain and satisfy Mapuche demands, lest they risk further conflict.[20]

Parlamentos in the eighteenth century also offered the Spanish and creole authorities a mechanism to promulgate trade, evangelize, and push crown policies that encouraged Mapuches to assimilate into European society in Araucanía. Although these strategies had been present since the first

Figure 1. Depiction of the 1873 Parlamento of Negrete with
Ambrosio O'Higgins. Illustrated by Claudio Gay, 1854.
Collection Biblioteca Nacional de Chile.

parlamento in Quillín in 1641, it took at least a century for the Spanish-
creoles to develop a strong colonial economy that depended in large part on
a good working relationship with the Mapuche, who had a considerable hold
on valuable trade goods, including cattle and salt. As mentioned previously,
conchavadores conducted trade in Araucanía and acted as intermediaries
between Mapuches and the colonial state.[21] Additionally, colonial adminis-
trators received valuable intelligence from missionaries and *capitanes de amigos* (creoles or mestizos who lived in Araucanía), who periodically reported
to crown officials any conflicts within Mapuche communities.[22] Nonetheless, all these mechanisms of Spanish control (conchavadores, missionaries,
capitanes de amigos) were carefully calibrated, and both sides benefited from
them.

The parlamento agreements always included (1) fealty and loyalty to the
king; (2) the promise to fight enemies of the king, who were now

automatically enemies of the Mapuche as well; (3) an agreement from the Mapuche to provide a certain number of their own as workers to the Spanish; (4) a pledge from the Mapuche to accept and listen to Catholic missionaries in their territories; and (5) an exchange of traditional gifts. Toward the end of the eighteenth century, when Spanish-creole influence in Araucanía was at its height, the governor held post-parlamento talks (also called juntas) with each butamalpu several days after the official parlamento ended to work through specific problems and solidify the parlamento agreements.[23]

The Parlamento of Negrete, held on February 13, 1726, provides an example of this constantly evolving relationship. There were twelve points of agreement in this parlamento. Of the twelve, the most significant were:

1. The Mapuche are to give up their arms.
2. The Mapuche are to become vassals of the king of Spain.
3. The Mapuche are enemies of the enemies of Spain.
5. The Mapuche will accept missionaries in Mapuche territory and comply with the Church if chosen to be baptized.
6. All kinds of problems persist in clandestine bartering. Therefore, *conchavos* (barters) are to be done freely but done in a public forum, such as a fair conducted three or four times yearly, with equal numbers of Indians and military personnel present.
7. Robberies of Mapuches within Indian territory are prohibited, and Spaniards are prohibited from conducting private negotiations in the interior of Mapuche territory.[24]

The term *vassal* dates to the Middle Ages and usually denotes a subject of a feudal lord who incurs both benefits and responsibilities as a result of that relationship. The *Diccionario de la lengua española* defines *vasallo* as "a king's subject or an individual with ties to vassalage" and "a person who recognizes his superior or is dependent upon him."[25] The above peace accords seem to confirm vassalage yet simultaneously allow for independence, particularly number 7, which clearly states that no robberies were to be committed within Indian territory and that no Spaniard was to negotiate privately within Mapuche territory. This seeming contradiction between being vassals of the king and concurrently being independent—while not an explicit contradiction—continues throughout the parlamentos held in the eighteenth century, and its ambiguity may help explain the differing perceptions that each party (Spanish and Mapuches) had at the negotiating table.

The language of vassalage persisted in the Tapihue Parlamento of 1774, which contains some interesting accords. The 1774 Tapihue Parlamento was also an agreement done under the auspices of the Bourbon monarch Charles III, known for his extensive and far-reaching reforms in Spanish America. According to one historian's analysis of this parlamento, the Bourbon crown, nervous about encroachment on Chilean territory from hostile powers (France, for example) and worried about how to control intertribal warfare among the different Mapuche groups, decided to elevate certain loyal, cooperative caciques and persecute caciques who were less willing to conform to crown expectations. The Spanish crown made allied caciques vassals, effectively bringing a group of Mapuches under Spanish law. Therefore, crimes such as the malón, rape, taking of captives, or murder became subject to prosecution. Additionally, the Bourbon crown allowed designated caciques and community leaders to control outbreaks of violence and the policing of their own communities, opening the door for the crown to "hispanize the territory controlled by the free men of Araucanía, converting Mapuches themselves into defenders of imperial order."[26]

The implication here was that now Spanish royal law took precedence over indigenous laws and customs. Therefore, caciques who were vassals of the Spanish were no longer part of an independent nation. But exactly what does this document mean by a nation? The text reflects ambivalence about defining a nation (nación) versus a nation-state (estado-nación).[27] For crown representatives at the parlamento, a nation was defined in colonial terms; that is, Mapuche territory and Mapuches themselves were contained as part of the colonial pact, politically speaking. The Mapuche, however, may have thought differently. Because the parlamentos are essentially Spanish documents, deciphering Mapuche intentions requires reading between the lines. I believe that for the Mapuche, a nation was as Donoso Rojas defined it: "a community of citizens living under the same regime or government and having a communion of interests; all inhabitants of a territory with traditions, aspirations and common interests."[28] For colonial officials, the political definition of a nation meant that Mapuches were "subordinated under a central authority that is charged with maintaining the unity of the group."[29] In other words, the Spanish crown defined a nation and a state identically, in a political sense, whereby it was the central authority and the Spanish legal system that provided the unity. So for the Spanish crown, Mapuches become vassals of the Spanish colonial nation-state. The distinct culture of the Mapuche, meanwhile, likely maintained a "nation" independent from, though perhaps allied with, Spain.

Problematic here is the interpretation of the 1774 parlamento. It is clear that Mapuches did not believe themselves to be vassals of the Spanish monarch. The *País Mapuche* blog, maintained by modern Mapuche-identified writers, argues that "the parlamentos coincided in recognizing the frontier at the Bío-Bío, that neither could cross without the permission of the other, differentiating in this way the territories and jurisdictions of both *pueblos* [communities]. It would concern, then, an international treaty among sovereign nations. In the last several years it has been supported by national as well as international instances.[30]

For example, accord 14 from the Parlamento of Tapihue of 1774 reads as follows: "No one can pass from now on except through the River passes at Santa Barbara, Purén, Nacimiento, Santa Juana and San Pedro, first presenting himself and be annotated in the Commanders' book, so that they know what goods are being returned to your Lands, bought or acquired with them, and also the guides who guide the Cavos . . . on the contrary, it will be taken as robbed all specimens and goods that do not pass through this quality control."[31]

The passage above is essentially a customs agreement whereby goods and men can utilize certain byways and all goods, guides, and merchants must pass through a checkpoint and register. There is a demarcation between *your* lands (Mapuche lands) and *our* lands (Spanish lands) and agreement that the Bío-Bío River is the border between the two. Furthermore, later in the same passage, it says that Mapuches must reciprocate with equal treatment if any Spaniard passes the river in the wrong place and does not register his goods, people, and so on. Thus what we have here is an agreement between two geographic entities that could be nations but that are politically defined as states. Why would a customs arrangement be necessary if Mapuches were vassals of the crown and therefore no longer a separate political state? The language of the parlamento treaties during this period seems to indicate that

Mapuches were, de facto, a separate nation-state, even though the Spanish crown at times represented the Mapuche as a politically and territorially subjugated people.

What complicates this picture is that at no time during the entire colonial period, and even into the early nineteenth century, were all Mapuche groups united as one political nation-state, making the Spanish colonial government's goal of subjugation almost impossible. Toward the end of the eighteenth century, the Spanish governor held juntas with each of the four butamalpus shortly after major parlamentos to solidify and implement the agreements made there. Parties to these juntas attempted to solve problems within their specific Mapuche groups. These juntas did not solidify Spanish control in the region; rather, they represented an effort to fracture ethnic control within and among the different Mapuche groups.

The testimony of Vicente Carvallo y Goyeneche demonstrates the ambiguity and the complexity of communication between Spanish officials and different Mapuche groups with whom they interacted at junta meetings. Carvallo y Goyeneche (1742–1816), born in Valdivia, witnessed several juntas between the Spanish authorities and Mapuche caciques. He had a long and distinguished military career that by 1788 had made him a captain. In 1790 he wrote *Historia de Chile* to "clarify the truth, confused in the passing of two and half centuries and darkened with fractured relations."[32] In this volume, Carvallo y Goyeneche describes several smaller juntas that took place in Santiago after the 1771 Negrete Parlamento.

Two juntas in particular stand out because of the Mapuche's "flippant" behaviors during the meetings, which could be attributed to the Mapuche's sense of their own autonomy. The first junta took place on December 13, 1772, and in attendance were forty caciques, fourteen *capitanejos* (indigenous captains), and 180 mocetones led by Major don Domingo Álvarez Ramírez. The goal of this junta was to reiterate the agreements that had been stipulated at the earlier Negrete Parlamento and to cease hostilities within Spanish territory. The Mapuche caciques present responded with "indifference . . . they were very condescending." Furthermore, they wanted to know what the "king paid because they hadn't left their country for their own benefit, but for trade that interested the Spanish and begged for by the governor."[33] The perceived arrogance of these Mapuches might well stem from a perception of their bargaining position that differed from that of the Spanish.

The second junta took place on November 21, 1772, also in Santiago. The *maestre de campo* (field master) convened this junta, in which the discussion revolved around the imposition of the death sentence to any Mapuche found committing crimes in Spanish territory, which was yet another reiteration of earlier peace agreements. To this, the caciques present responded by drinking a lot of wine, getting drunk, and returning to their lands. They treated this junta with the same "indifference as with the others, and with a type of insensibility with which they conduct themselves with any kind of serious issue. They are convinced that these assemblies are a lavish reception for them to eat and get drunk."[34] Rather than a demonstration of bad manners, these Mapuche caciques may have been asserting jurisdiction over their own people, including their prerogative to define criminal behavior and mete out punishment.

Given that this is a Spanish source, it is not surprising that Carvallo y Goyeneche describes Mapuches as drunken, careless, and irresponsible. However, these same behaviors may very well have been a strategy that Mapuches utilized to express their confidence and security in knowing that the Spanish really did not have the power to enforce these agreements. Therefore Mapuches felt safe enough to get drunk and go back to their territory. Their "condescending" attitude and "indifference" amounted to a specific collective attitude that Mapuches knew garnered results. That is, they realized that they could return to their lands without reprisals on the part of the Spanish and that these agreements were only binding if both parties believed in the necessity to keep them. Consequently, these seemingly careless and irresponsible behaviors on the part of the Mapuche representatives present at these two junta meetings may have been calculated, sovereignty-affirming behaviors.

Interestingly, Ambrosio O'Higgins (father of Bernardo O'Higgins), governor-general of Chile, disliked Carvallo y Goyeneche. In a report in 1790, O'Higgins complained that Carvallo y Goyeneche had requested "a three-year leave that was only six months" to write a history that others more qualified than he had already written, and that he had embellished his writings to excuse himself from his rightful duties on the frontier.[35] By claiming that Carvallo y Goyeneche had exaggerated about his time serving on the frontier, O'Higgins effectively cast doubt on Carvallo y Goyeneche's interpretations of the crown's frontier relations with Mapuches, including the junta meetings. Carvallo y Goyeneche's perceptions of the juntas, however, do reveal attitudes toward the Mapuche among certain functionaries of the crown.

Carvallo y Goyeneche's history also hints at the deep ambiguities of the parlamentos in the eighteenth century. These meetings served several functions, and they almost certainly were not perceived in the same way across ethnic lines. For Mapuches, the parlamentos were large gatherings that brought together several Mapuche subgroups that collectively represented a separate indigenous nation-state—although not necessarily a united one—to air their grievances and negotiate peace with the Spanish colonial state. For the Spaniards, the parlamentos were meetings among vassals of the same nation, some more privileged than others. The parlamentos (and the junta meetings that followed them) became the mechanism by which the Spanish colonial state negotiated territory, vassalage, and attempts at Christianization and incorporation into Spanish colonial European society. The Mapuche groups utilized the parlamentos as bargaining chips in inter-Mapuche conflicts, as well as to effectively keep the Spanish from outright controlling Araucanía. Eighteenth-century parlamentos might have brought the two factions to the same bargaining and feasting tables, but they did not signify the same goals and expectations to both sides.

Parlamentos in the Nineteenth Century

The dynamic of the parlamentos changed in the nineteenth century as the emergent Chilean state supplanted Spanish rule. The negotiating parties were no longer vassals of the same colonial empire but a dominant state and a subjugated state negotiating not just peace and trade but also incorporation. One implicit goal of the Chilean state in the nineteenth-century parlamentos was to subjugate the Mapuche to Spanish-creole society. The upheavals of independence necessitated a different attitude toward Araucanía and its inhabitants. The nascent Chilean state pursued aggressive geographic expansion, seeking to solidify the nation-state and its borders. The inherent conflict of interest between the nineteenth-century Mapuche and the Chilean creoles provides a potential explanation for why the Spaniards found a welcome audience in Araucanía during the independence wars and la guerra a muerte in the 1820s. Moreover, the chaos of this period pitted different Mapuche groups against each other, with some supporting the creole forces against Spain and others becoming royalists.

Antonio Varas, a visitor to Araucanía in 1848, wrote that under colonial rule the Spaniards and Mapuches followed certain rules and that both believed ultimate authority belonged to the king of Spain. After independence, new conflicts arose between the Chilean Republic and the Mapuche as the withdrawal of Spain left a sovereignty vacuum. For Varas, bringing Mapuches to submission violently was only going to encourage resistance on their part. In his writings, he recommended developing a system based on the colonial model, arguing that "it was important to civilize the Indians by peaceful means, that education and evangelization were the most viable means to achieve the definitive incorporation of its inhabitants to the national territory."[36] In post-independence society, therefore, the Chilean Republic was to administer Araucanía under the same principles that had proved successful previously.[37] Hence the state held parlamentos with rebellious Mapuches and brought back missionaries, but it never digressed from its goal of forcing indigenous peoples to be subjugated to creole/Chilean society.

Until the 1830s, the state's official policy toward Mapuches consisted of maintaining a frontier army and subsidizing friendly Mapuche caciques, such as Lorenzo Colipí, who died in 1838.[38] Beginning in the 1840s, the advance of commerce and the introduction of wheat for the world market spurred the construction of railroads and brought immigration to Chile. New settlers seeking economic opportunity pushed south of the Bío-Bío River into frontier territory, where they labored on the railroads and the new wheat-producing haciendas. Mapuche lands were very fertile and good for wheat production and were therefore lucrative in the eyes of the state. Mapuches themselves were not willing to relinquish them, precipitating the Chilean state's enticements, which some caciques took, and outright threats, such as land seizures. By 1858 there were fourteen thousand new settlers in Araucanía, upsetting the delicate balance between Mapuches and the Chilean government.[39] In 1853 Chile created the new province of Arauco, which theoretically covered the entire frontier district of Araucanía.[40] By the late 1850s, the intendant of Arauco, Colonel Cornelio Saavedra, had proposed a new policy that consisted of "the gradual occupation of Araucanian territory by moving the official frontier south by stages, establishing new lines of forts."[41]

Colonel Saavedra's "new" policy, which became known as the final pacification of the Mapuche and Araucanía, took more than twenty years to accomplish. By 1868 the frontier settlements of Mulchen and Angol existed and the frontier line had been moved to the Malleco River, with more forts along the coast. Cacique Colipán, then leader of the Mapuche, mounted assaults and counterattacks through 1871, whereby the Mapuche managed to maintain control over a large swath of territory until their final defeat in 1883.[42] During this period, prominent newspapers expounded on the need for "law and order" on the frontier. Their arguments included the following: "One has to conclude once and for all with that 'interminable conquest' of the barbarians that have cost us so much and killed so many. The government has left Araucanía in a state of abandonment that compromises the honor of the Chilean Republic. . . . The Araucanians constitute a nation and therefore can negotiate peace treaties with foreign nations."[43]

The Chilean state's acknowledgment of Mapuche autonomy and perhaps outright sovereignty over Araucanía complicated the strategies its leaders utilized to subdue the Mapuche and claim frontier territory as Chilean owned and controlled. Although Saavedra's policy was touted as being new, it differed very little from previous ones. The continual push southward had begun as early as the colonial period. The difference in the mid-nineteenth century was that Mapuches had comparatively less success at protecting their lands and their culture against the state's continuing onslaught and superior resources. By the 1850s, it was clear that Mapuches were not going to be good citizens, vis-à-vis Chilean/European elite notions of citizenry, beginning the decades-long villainizing of the Mapuche, the subsequent efforts at outright colonization, and, finally, war and subjugation. Independence leaders (except Bernardo O'Higgins) were reluctant to have Mapuches as their citizen brothers. They could perhaps accept them verbally, but few treated Mapuches as citizens in practice. Creole elites, in fact, never deviated from their racist notions of Mapuches at any point either during the colonial period or after independence, as witnessed by the state's brutal treatment of them during the violent era of the 1820s. After independence, Chile's leaders formally declared in the constitution of 1822, and again in the constitutions of 1828 and 1833, that all territory clear down to Cape Horn, including Araucanía, now belonged to the Chilean state. In other words, rhetoric aside, politics, economics, land, and culture prevented Chile's leaders from fully accepting Mapuches on their own terms. In a sense Chile had always intended to sub-jugate the Mapuche and Araucanía, and it finally did so in the second half of the century.

In 1803 representatives of the Spanish crown, including Ambrosio O'Higgins and high-ranking indigenous officials—such as loncos and other caciques who represented the four butamalpus that composed the "Mapuche nation"—celebrated a parlamento in Negrete, known as the General Parla-mento of Negrete.[44] This parlamento demonstrated new features that fore-shadowed the coming of independence and the eventual outcome of the Tapihue Parlamento of 1825. The parlamento questioned the definition of "nation" and, ultimately, the appropriateness of the concept for creoles and Mapuches.

The introductory paragraph of the Parlamento of Negrete of 1803 is instruc-tive: "This is an International Treaty, because in it there are established lin-eages and obligations between Imperial Spain and a Pre-Columbian Nation, aside from being a true Treaty by a complete nation (by the significant geo-graphical representation of its authorities). . . . In this [agreement] the internal sovereignty of the Mapuche Community for the defense of its territory and the maintenance of its economic and social life according to the autochthonous customs of each of the Butamalpus is established. Furthermore, external sov-ereignty between them and Spain has been agreed upon."[45]

This introduction represents Araucanía and the Spanish colonial state in Chile as two separate nation-states able to treat with one another. The par-lamento continues with eight separate peace accords that discuss traditional issues such as trade and missions. Two accords, however, are worth pointing out. Accord 3 instructs that "children of Governors, Caciques or Principal Indians, receive a Christian education at the Propaganda Fide School in the city of Chillán." The accord asserts that the advantages of such cross-cultural schooling "include experience in already having various sons of the natives of the four Butamalpus placed with the dignity and veneration of the priests there."[46] The Spanish crown's aim to evangelize Mapuches was apparent in this parlamento, but it took it one step further by *requiring* that sons of important Mapuche caciques be educated at the Propaganda Fide School. During the chaos of the independence years, it was precisely these educated sons who remained loyal to the Spanish crown. Ironically, Spain's attempt at evangelization perhaps worked too well, since it was exactly these same Mapuches who rejected independence and sought to maintain their autonomy from the newly created Chilean state.

Accord 6 reinforces the notion that, at least for the purposes of the 1803 Negrete Parlamento, the Spanish viewed Mapuches from the four butamalpus as a *separate nation*. This accord discusses Mapuche loyalty to the Spanish crown through vassalage, which, as previously noted, was not novel, since vassalage was a common aspect of parlamentos throughout the colonial period. However, this accord warns Mapuches that grave consequences would result from "treating with some nations whose sole purpose is to destroy its inhabitants while becoming owners of the land, which experience has already demonstrated, adding that in the case of war with any foreign nation, they should be obliged as good vassals to personally come to the defense of His Majesty's dominions as long as they are attacked, which the four Butamalpus have confirmed and sworn they would do."[47] In this case, Mapuche vassals of the king were not allowed to let foreign nations land on the coast of Mapuche territory because the Spanish warned that these nations would take *their* lands (Mapuche lands) from them!

Commerce and trade in large part determined the Mapuche's willingness to collaborate or negotiate with the Chilean state. Autonomy—or at least equity—was another determinant, one that became an increasingly difficult issue as the century progressed, as Mapuche lands became more appealing to the ruling creole elite for expansion. Add increasing economic output and immigration, and this panorama served to put Mapuches on the defensive once again.

The parlamento held between Commander José de Susso, emissary of José de San Martín, then governor of Cuyo Province on the Argentinean side of the Andes cordillera, and sixteen Pehuenche caciques on October 23, 1814, near the Planchón Pass (between what is now Mendoza, Argentina, and central Chile), provides an example. At this parlamento, Susso, through his interpreter, Father Francisco Inalikang, requested that the Pehuenches "watch the passes and resist the enemies, and that if they attempt to cross to this side of the Cordillera, that the Pehuenches will give immediate notice to the frontier." Their reward would be to "do business" (*comerciar*) in Chile, and they would be protected in Mendoza.[48] In another parlamento, in

January 1817, once again the Pehuenches were asked to not allow adversaries to cross the Andes. The tone of this meeting can be seen in the following excerpt:

> In the following month, the Caciques began to approach the Fort of San Carlos with all the displays of a savage life, bringing to the rearguard of their people of war, their wives and children. Arriving there with their own, General San Martín kindly offered them a glass of wine before entering into negotiations; but not one of them accepted, stating that if they drank, they would not have the necessary state of mind to focus their due consideration on the matter about to be discussed. Then the interpreter, who was Father Francisco Inalikang, monk from San Francisco, made a speech to the Indians, warning them that they were called upon by the General to a solemn conference, and offering them some drinks and gifts, he asked them for permission to let his army pass through Pehuenche territory to attack the Spanish, *that they were foreigners whose intentions and purposes were aimed at stripping them of their lands, robbing them of their cattle, and taking away their wives and children.* Not all the Caciques believed this cunning trick, and it was only used for passing two or three shipments to Talca and Curicó, getting the attention of the royalists and proceeding differently.[49]

Chilean rhetoric, which essentially accused Spaniards of doing what the Chilean creoles intended to do to Mapuche lands, appears to have worked. Indeed, after all the deliberations, wine, and speeches, Cacique Nincollancu told San Martín "that the Pehuenches, with the exception of three Caciques, accepted his propositions."[50] Ironically, after independence it was the newly formed Chilean state, rather than the Spanish crown, that worked to strip the Mapuche of their lands and rob them of their cattle.

Mapuche strategies also differed in the nineteenth century. Gone were the "flippant" behaviors of acting carelessly and getting drunk at parlamentos and juntas and then returning to their lands with the surety that Spanish officials would be hard-pressed to retaliate. Now Mapuche groups, and in the case above, the Pehuenches, refused the drinks offered because the ceremonial ritual had been stripped of meaning. Patriots like San Martín and others now posed a much bigger threat to Mapuche independence than the Spanish had throughout the colonial period.

Tapihue Parlamento of 1825

The Parlamento of Tapihue of 1825 was markedly different from previous parlamentos in several ways, and it represented a turning point in Chilean–Mapuche relations. First, unlike parlamentos in the colonial period, in which the different Mapuche groups sent caciques and other important indigenous personnel, along with hundreds of warriors and interpreters to represent them, only one cacique attended Tapihue in 1825, Francisco Mariluán. This Spanish-educated cacique represented fourteen indigenous communities, now called reducciones. Under this parlamento, for the first time, Mapuches were not treated as a separate nation-state. As accord 1 states, "Both authorities, convinced of the great benefits of becoming one family, and to oppose the enemies of *our* country [emphasis mine] in order to increase and consolidate trade, and to desist from all the evils that have befallen the Republic in fourteen consecutive years of fighting, don Mariluán has come as a representative of all the Caciques to become united in opinion and the rights of the grand Chilean family."[51]

By limiting the number of delegates to the parlamento, the Chilean government explicitly makes the point that Mapuches are no longer a separate nation-state but a marginalized group within the Chilean nation-state. Furthermore, the language of the above passage is instructive. Not only did the 1825 accord fail to consider the Mapuche as a separate nation-state politically, as they had always believed themselves to be, but it refused to recognize the subdivisions (Pehuenches, Arribanos, and so on) within the indigenous nation-state under the new Chilean jurisdiction. Their existence, moreover, now depended on their cooperation and consolidation under the banner of one cacique, thus becoming part of a "grand Chilean family." Hence Mapuches were now, as accord 3 specifies, "Chilean citizens, with all the prerogatives, grace, and privileges that correspond to them."[52]

Yet the parlamento accords also contradict themselves regarding the issues of Mapuche statehood and citizenship. For example, accord 18 says that "governors and caciques . . . will not permit that any Chilean exist in the *territories under their domain*, and in this way to better maintain the peace, union, and security of these new *brothers*."[53] If Mapuches were to be part of the "grand Chilean family," it would stand to reason that they would be regarded as full Chilean citizens. Accord 18, however, seems to claim that Mapuches are still not Chilean citizens and that they are still masters of their own lands—lands that are now part of the Chilean state. In fact, accord 2 specifically delineates the exact geographical boundaries of what constitutes Chilean national territory: "The Chilean Republic's territory spans from the depopulated Atacama until the limits of Chiloé province,"[54] which includes all of Araucanía. These are promises the Chilean Republic never kept.[55]

Subsequent peace agreements (often called tratados rather than parlamentos) treated the Mapuche as a conquered group that had little power to resist state demands. The ritualistic aspect of parlamentos, very much diminished beginning with Tapihue in 1825, ceased to exist altogether in subsequent agreements. Later agreements had few Mapuches in attendance, no ritualistic speeches, and little to no food or drink. Even the language of the agreements was sparser, with no preambles and few if any accords. As an example, Cornelio Saavedra, creator of the Pacification Plan of Araucanía, which he initiated in 1861 and continued from 1867 to 1869, with a parlamento in 1870, held a parlamento with the Arribanos in 1867 that lasted a little more than two hours, with no definitive conclusion. Shortly after, Saavedra threatened the Arribanos, saying that "if they did not meet and come to an agreement with him within that afternoon or the next day, he would mount an attack on them. . . . They [the Abajinos] commissioned Pailahueque to come to an agreement with the *huinca* (Creole) commander."[56]

At least two parlamentos took place between 1869 (Parlamento of Toltén) and 1870 (Parlamento of Ipinca). There, Saavedra sought to obtain various concessions from the Mapuche groups represented. At the 1869 Parlamento of Toltén, Saavedra bribed the caciques with bushels of wheat to feed their people, who had been on the brink of starvation: "There was much misery within those tribes and some wheat was given to them, assuring them that more help would be forthcoming on the day of the parlamento."[57] At Ipinca a year later, the parlamento resulted in a strained military alliance between the state and the Arribanos, who refused to abide by an earlier agreement to have the boundary line moved to the Toltén River and accept repopulation of the city of Villarica. The consequences of the Arribanos' refusal to abide by earlier agreements were continued warfare that culminated in their eventual defeat.[58]

Nonetheless, there were some exceptions that are eerily like the parlamentos held before independence. On March 4, 1860, for example, Chilean authorities held a junta general with several caciques in Tucapel. This junta had eight accords, some of which read like a peace treaty between two separate nation-states. The first accord delineates the boundaries of Indian territory, divided into four administrative units. The accord does not state that the territory belongs to the Chilean Republic. Rather, it delimits the exact boundaries in which these particular Mapuches are to reside: "The limits of the territory will be the cordillera Nahuelbuta to the East and to the West, the ocean."[59] The four named caciques are called governors, with assistants and a captain commissar of war. Additionally, the government agrees to pay these cacique governors and their assistants a salary of 110 pesos, and the captain commissar of war a salary of 60 pesos.[60] The same political organization took place in the Tapihue Tratado of 1825.

Paying caciques salaries was not new; Spanish crown officials also paid certain caciques salaries as essentially "state" employees during the colonial period. Accord 3 discusses a licensing agreement for all "Spaniards" (creoles) who wished to reside in the territory. The cacique governors kept the licenses, and if they allowed Spaniards to reside in the territory under their jurisdiction without licenses, they were responsible for any crimes unlicensed persons committed. Accord 6 allows for the movement of troops in the territory, with cacique governors responsible for their maintenance.[61] The latter half of the junta general considers the war debt of twenty-five thousand pesos that the cacique governors owed the state and notes that the cacique governors' lands "are held as collateral until their owners satisfy the costs to each of them after the lands have been equally divided amongst them. During the period in which these lands are held in collateral they would be at the disposition of the Caciques Governors so that they may use them for the good of the poor or of all those who solicit permission to harvest or place animals on them."[62] This junta (not parlamento) reflects both the old ways of treating with the Mapuche and the new. Although the cacique governors had autonomy within their respective territories, it was also clear from this junta that they were no longer owners of that territory. In fact, they were now obligated to pay twenty-five thousand pesos in damages against land the state parceled out to them—land that used to belong to them.

In July 1871, Colonel José Francisco Gana held a *tratado de paz* (peace treaty) with Cacique Faustino Quilahueque as representative of the Arribanos in Collipulli. This tratado has nine accords. There is no mention of territorial boundaries in any of the accords. Accord 1 discusses the caciques handing over their male children to the intendant of Arauco to be educated in Santiago, with visits home once a year. Accord 2 discusses the exchange of prisoners on both sides. Like the junta general of 1860, accord 3 discusses the use of licenses by those deemed to be of "Spanish race." Accord 4 mandates that those who choose to do business in Indian territory must have a passport issued by the caciques.[63] One would assume that the use of passports denotes passage from one country to another, but it seems that in this case, the passports serve more as identifiers of those conducting trade in Araucanía who are not Mapuches, in itself interesting since the lands within Araucanía were now part of the national territorial boundary.

These later tratados, therefore, unlike their predecessors prior to 1825, worked under the Chilean state's assumption that the Mapuche communities it negotiated with inhabited lands that belonged to the Chilean state and not to Mapuches. Mapuches were now allowed to use the lands but did not outright own them. Although the Chilean state repeatedly says in these agreements that Mapuches were Chilean citizens, the explicit use of passports and licenses to denote who is Spanish (Chilean) and who is Mapuche seems to indicate that that Mapuche did not have the same rights and privileges as Chileans and thus could not be fully part of the "Chilean family."[64] These tratados were, therefore, no longer peace treaties between two separate nation-states but rather the Chilean state asserting its authority over a conquered territory and people.

Conclusion

In the nineteenth century, parlamentos maintained some of their traditional functions, but they shifted in scope and meaning. They were still seen as a means, along with missions, to bring about peace. Ceremonies with plenty of food, alcohol, and gift giving continued in the early part of the nineteenth century but stopped abruptly after 1825. Changes occurred in the objectives of the parlamentos, which after 1825 were rarely named as such. Instead of being fully fledged negotiations between independent nations, most agreements were either tratados or juntas by which the privileged Chilean nation dictated terms to a subordinate ethnic group. Chilean leaders wanted Mapuche lands to expand the Chilean state southward, and the parlamentos changed to make room for that goal. As a consequence, Mapuches were no longer considered equal partners at these meetings. Instead, they became explicitly second-class citizens[65] who were only permitted to negotiate because they had done so for several hundred years.

Illustrative of this point is a conversation that Ignacio Domeyko, a Polish scientist, mineralogist, and educator, had with an elderly Mapuche cacique during his travels in Araucanía in 1845. The conversation took place in a llano dotted by three crosses, where sixteen caciques gathered to welcome him to their lands. The elderly cacique, whom Domeyko described as "of athletic stature and with a ponderous voice," said, "Here, in this place . . . for many years we have celebrated peace with the Spanish; the crosses that you see are testimony to this; and that we have respected until now—we want peace and we will guard it faithfully, just like our forefathers did."[66] By the mid-nineteenth century, the parlamentos persisted mainly as a form of cultural memory, a tradition that recalled an era in which the Mapuche had the power to negotiate with Spain and the sovereignty that made relatively peaceful coexistence possible.

CHAPTER SIX

Notions of Chilean Citizenship

CHILE'S HISTORY IN THE NINETEENTH CENTURY IS RICH IN ITS chronicling of state formation. Many of Chile's historians were themselves architects of the nation-state, either as statesmen, politicians, or army generals. Quite a few foreigners also came to the long, thin country to explore and write about it. This chapter explores the views of several nineteenth-century Chilean creole elites (including politicians, historians, and explorers) on citizenship and what citizenship meant in the nineteenth-century context of modernity. Its focus is on how and why citizenship was important to Chile's state-building project and, furthermore, how Mapuches and their place in this new republic were crucial to what Chile as a nation-state became in the modern world of the nineteenth century. Although many of these writers believed that Mapuches had no place in the new Republic of Chile, some were not convinced that they were either heroes or barbaric. The importance of these views underscores inherent racism, and this elite rhetoric fueled the state's war against the Mapuche population.

The establishment of the Chilean Republic had two main goals: conquest of all lands, and dealing with the Mapuche Indian problem. Chilean elites grappled with how to accomplish these twin goals, mixed with their feelings and philosophies about exactly who Mapuches were and how to incorporate them into mainstream Chilean society. The result was the slow overtaking of ancestral Mapuche lands through manipulation (selling of lands) and force (outright war). Mapuches were to become part of Chilean society but on Chilean elites' terms—not on Mapuche terms. As we have seen, some Mapuche groups capitulated to state demands and were well rewarded. Others chose to defend their lands and autonomy from state encroachment. Because of the fragmented nature of intra-Mapuche ethnic relations (which the state used to its advantage) Mapuches lost sight of their goal of maintaining control over their native lands and continued to fight with each other as well as with the Chilean state. In this protracted process, they became second-class citizens in their own lands.

After Chile's independence from Spain, territorial acquisition and populating these newly acquired territories with Chilean citizens defined the Chilean Republic's physical territory. Now that monarchical rule no longer applied, Chilean leaders identified themselves as representatives of the sovereign public composed of citizens, and citizenship legally differentiated the new state from a monarchical state composed of subjects. But how was citizenship defined and who exactly was a citizen in nineteenth-century Chile? The answers depended on who asked the questions. For many Chilean elites, a citizen had specific characteristics that were European in origin. A citizen was a man who had certain qualities (owned land, was literate, had respectability within his community) and who played an active role in politics—that is, voted. Clearly, Chilean elites believed Mapuches did not possess these attributes. "Being a citizen implie[d] being an active member of the State, and influencing his political future through an alleged vote, which would develop a valuable link between the State and the people. In other words, as a 'man,' he's an individual and a member of his community. Therefore, as a 'man,' a citizen may refer himself to a specific group: *la patria* [the fatherland]."[1]

Chilean intellectuals and visitors to nineteenth-century Chile wrote extensively about not just citizenship but also the concept of *gran familia*, nation, national identity, and Mapuches. These concepts were significant because they influenced how Chile's leaders chose to implement governmental policies that effectively either excluded Mapuches or made them second-class citizens on their own lands. Sarah Chambers argues that la gran familia was the number-one marker for citizenship in the newly established Chilean Republic. "Paternal authority and responsibility" were central to the notion of nation building in Chile.[2] "By providing for diverse Chileans, [these] paternalist policies contributed to state hegemony, but they also prioritized patrician responsibilities over citizen rights."[3] Similarly, James Wood argues that nation or national identity was a moving target during the early national period because Chileans were just trying to figure out who they were. "The nation, *la patria*, was the entire community of Chileans and their corresponding *chilenidad*."[4] Furthermore, "nation was also the carrier of culture" emphasizing that in Chile, like elsewhere in Latin America during the nineteenth century, citizenship was problematized through race.[5] Nonetheless, family-centered policies tended to be more locally implemented with the lower classes. Citizenship, therefore, although granted to most elite and former soldiers' families who repented, did not necessarily apply to others, including Mapuches.

There were differences between those elites who espoused a form of republicanism and those who professed liberalism. Liberalism allowed for forgetting or refusing to throw out the past, whereas republicanism was more in line with "the absence of arbitrary domination"—that is, colonialism's authority. For historian Bárbara Silva Avaria, these political notions were, above all, excuses for the elite to rule.[6] Citizenship, then, was by definition restrictive, and Mapuches did not fit these descriptions because they were not seen as "civilized" and capable of living in an "enlightened" or European community. In this sense, Chile was in step with most other Latin American countries in the post-independence period, regarding the United States and Europe as models of political enlightenment and modernization. In the second half of the century, Argentina waged a bloody war of extermination against its indigenous population to usurp their lands and to expand its fast-growing export-led production of wheat. The government's excuse for inciting war was that the Indians were barbarians and incapable of becoming proper citizens of Argentina. "For the Argentine elites, indigenous citizenship was a paradox best solved, as Deputy Molina implied, by the complete elimination of these awkward 'citizens,' perhaps by drowning."[7]

What makes the Chilean case interesting is that most Chilean elites, no matter how racist, had a stake in incorporating the Mapuche and thus wanted to address the Mapuche "problem" as soon as possible. Again, Araucanía and its Mapuche inhabitants become a central focus of the Chilean government's state-building project.

To be sure, not all Chilean intellectuals and elites believed Mapuches to be uncivilized barbarians. Joanna Crow makes this argument in *The Mapuche in Modern Chile*: "I would argue that elite attitudes toward the contemporary Mapuche (or Araucanian) could be as varied as those toward his heroic ancestors. In opposition to the savage, rebel Indian, who presented a major obstacle to the consolidation of the modern nation-state, for example, was the 'civilized' (or at least partially civilized) loyal Indian who had earned his place as a citizen of the Chilean republic."[8] She argues that class as much as race had an influence on perceptions of Mapuches as members (or possible members) of Chilean society. The examples she provides from newspapers, like the prominent *El Mercurio*, describe some Mapuches, such as the famous Juan Colipí, as having "prominent cheekbones, a penetrating and alert stare, and full lips; he wears a black, wide-brimmed hat and a silk scarf around his neck; apart from that his clothes are no different from those of his compatriots."[9] Another description she cites comes from the southern newspaper *El Araucano*: "What beautiful Indians! Tall, athletic, with their heads held high, a pink if not white complexion, and riding fine horses."[10] These examples describe the physical features of these Mapuches as similar to those of Chilean elites themselves, thus European. The whiter the complexion and the more European the clothes (the silk scarf and hat), not only the wealthier but more Europeanized, and therefore more Chilean, were these Mapuches. Wealth may have been a factor, as Crowe rightfully points out, but racial features (tall, prominent cheekbones; pink or white complexion; and so on), as well as the adoption of European cultural norms, were much more indicative of a Mapuche being modern and progressive, and a far cry from the half-clothed, bloodthirsty warrior who was more typically described. So these wealthy, progressive, and modern Mapuches were more European and therefore more acceptable, potential citizens-in-the-making.

Not all Chilean intellectuals, both conservatives and liberals, wrote about the Mapuche. For those that did, their views were very much tied to their political and philosophical viewpoints, and most followed a decidedly liberal path. Liberals during this period believed that indigenous peoples were, by definition, "uncivilized" and "barbarians." The path toward respectability required education and, for some, the adoption of Christian norms. Beginning in the 1840s, prominent Chilean historians and intellectuals, such as the exiled Venezuelan Andrés Bello, who founded the University of Chile in 1842, and José Victorino Lastarria, a founding member and leader of the intellectual movement of 1842, worked to educate young men in the nineteenth-century liberal tradition. This intellectual ferment found outlets in newspapers (*El Semanario de Santiago*) and the Literary Society with Lastarria as director.[11]

For liberals and conservatives alike, Mapuches could become members of Chilean society only if they assimilated, and thus became less "barbaric." For example, Diego Barros Arana (1830–1907), one of Chile's most famous nineteenth-century historians, is best known for his monumental sixteen-volume *Historia Jeneral de Chile*. He was a liberal and positivist thinker, a faculty member in the humanities at the University of Chile, a post he had held since 1855. In 1871 he became dean of the School of Humanities. He was rector of the university from 1893 to 1897. Arana had very negative and racist views of the Mapuche. In particular, he believed Mapuches to be barbarians and uncivilized; therefore they were unable to take advantage of their fertile lands. "In other words, the Indians did not deserve the good lands that they traditionally inhabited, and these lands need to be 'conveniently exploited' in order to achieve a higher degree of agricultural production destined for the feeding of the population and for export."[12] Additionally, Barros Arana believed Mapuches were incapable of modern work methods because of their insistence on the division of labor and because they had no effective government (at least not one based on the liberal European model that Barros Arana favored). Because they farmed their land communally, Mapuches were not qualified to become private property owners, which as a liberal, Barros Arana preferred and considered superior to any other form of land ownership. To Barros Arana, communal land ownership inhibited material and industrial progress. Lastly, the Mapuche lacked spiritual development and were inferior religiously because of their belief in many gods and their lackluster record of conversion to Catholicism. Barros Arana did advocate for change among the Mapuche, if that change came through education at the hands of a more advanced society and state, "and this is an important point in nineteenth-century liberal thought: these societies were able to change in a positive manner as long as they were influenced by a superior and dominant 'civilization.'"[13]

Some liberals believed that the Mapuche did not deserve citizenship of any kind because they were incapable of incorporation, either through education or any other type of state-run program. The most famous example was Benjamín Vicuña Mackenna. In his early years, he fought in the civil war of

1851 on the side of the liberals. He was arrested, and the Council of War proceeded to condemn him to death but eventually commuted his sentence to imprisonment. After living in exile for three years, he returned and continued to work against the conservative regimes in power since 1833.[14] In 1865 the university administration asked Vicuña Mackenna to write about la guerra a muerte (1819–1824). The argument for revisiting these years stemmed from the administration's desire to see a more honorable treatment of the terrible events during this period. "National historians had neglected the study of the last activities of the caudillos that, between the Ñuble and Valdivia, had hoisted the King's banner."[15] University officials may have been hoping for historical justification for the state's current war against the Mapuche in Araucanía.

In 1868 the House of Deputies fiercely debated the issue of Araucanía and the Mapuche. In keeping with his anticivilizing outlook toward the Mapuche, Vicuña Mackenna wanted and argued for their destruction because of their "naturally violent nature." Unlike the colonial period, when the Spanish crown lacked the resources to colonize Mapuches, Mackenna contended, the state had plenty of resources. He provided an example from 1835, when a little more than three hundred men fought and won a battle against the powerful Mapuche caciques Maguil and Colipí, who had held an uprising in Araucanía on October 2. Most important to Mackenna was that government forces lost only two men and rescued more than three hundred captives while killing hundreds of Mapuches.[16] For Mackenna, this example proved that the "Indians, who many invoke their rights to the law, are nothing but bandits and highway robbers."[17] At the same session, he further asserted that the Indian was brave but that all savages were and "it is true that the Indian defends his ground; but he defends it because he hates civilization, hates the law, the priesthood, education. The homeland that he defends is that of his freedom and bloody idleness, not the holy homeland of the heart, the heritage of our elders, sanctified by her laws, her traditions and her graves."[18] In the August 14 session, "Vicuña Mackenna continued to insist on the session's previous ideas, signaling particularly the fact that the cruel nature of the Indian only made it submit after a severe lesson."[19] Hence, for Vicuña Mackenna, the only path ahead in Araucanía was the complete annihilation of the Mapuche, nothing more and nothing less.

In 1868 Vicuña Mackenna wrote *La guerra a muerte*[20] in fulfillment of the university's request of three years earlier. This work centered on the state's ability to defeat the ailing Spanish army and crush the Mapuche in the early years of the 1820s. According to Vicuña Mackenna, the state achieved the first objective with the death of Juan Manuel Pico, the last Spanish commander, in October 1824. The decapitation of Pico put to a definitive end, finally, the war to the death. "From this day forward, said one of the soldiers who had carried out the order, the Indians have finally begun to calm down."[21] Three months later, in January 1825, a parlamento between the state and all the Mapuche reducciones took place in Tapihue (see chapter 5). It concluded with the first peace agreement since Chile's creoles had declared independence fifteen years earlier.[22] Thus, for Vicuña Mackenna, "Chile, in all her abundance and magnificent unity, reclaimed officially her true name of Nation, and took her sovereign place among the rest of the nations of the universe."[23]

Renewed conflict between the state and the Mapuche in the late 1850s culminated in Saavedra's frontier policy, which exacerbated existing conflicts between Mapuches and the state as well as within Mapuche communities themselves, weakening their resistance to state encroachment. The outbreak of war between the Chilean state and the Mapuche during this period further destabilized already fragile intra-Mapuche alliances, which ended with their final defeat in 1883. In *La guerra a muerte* Vicuña Mackenna argued that the conquest of the frontier had been part of the Chilean state's goal since independence. Conquering and "civilizing" the Mapuche, in his view, was part of *chilenidad*. *La guerra a muerte*, then, like other historical writings of the period, becomes a narrative that links the early conquest of Araucanía with the independence wars and the founding myths of the nation.

By restoring and glorifying the state's role in this war, Vicuña Mackenna also justified political policy toward the Mapuche. The image of Mapuches as both savage and passive—easily swayed by foreign influence and thus not masters of their own destiny—was powerful. Both attitudes justified the state's Mapuche policy of conquest and subjugation by denying the Indian (and his "naturally violent nature") both dignity and agency. As a nationalistic narrative, therefore, *La guerra a muerte*, by providing a useful tool for creating the "best" Indian policy to combat the problems in Araucanía, established political unity between liberals and conservatives and served as the basis for the Indian policies Vicuña Mackenna advocated for in the 1868 congressional debates.

Other liberal intellectuals of the period were not as extreme as Vicuña Mackenna, preferring to forge a middle ground whereby the Mapuche could, through modeling behavior and good communication, be incorporated into Chilean society. One such writer was Francisco Bilbao (1823–1865), a liberal philosopher (an extreme radical to some) who lived most of his short life in exile for his radical beliefs on popular sovereignty and his anticlerical stance on the church, which after the civil war of 1829–1830 severely conflicted with the ultra-conservative Portalian state. Bilbao's most famous work, *Sociabilidad Chilena* (1844), caused an upheaval and resulted in Bilbao being put on trial, as well as his expulsion from the Instituto Nacional without a degree.[24] In addition to severely criticizing the Catholic Church, *Sociabilidad Chilena* advocated for public education and private property.

Bilbao ultimately believed Mapuches needed to be civilized and incorporated into Chilean society, and in 1847 he wrote *Los Araucanos* while exiled in Paris. Unlike other liberals, such as Barros Arana, he did not hesitate to criticize the Chilean state's methods in achieving this lofty goal. In *Los Araucanos* he argued that the Chilean state, by continuing to war with the Mapuche, was in effect becoming just like them: "The frontier Chileans have taken something from the Araucanos [Mapuches] and our governments' ignorance permits a war of savages. Burning their ranches and their properties, killing them without mercy, fomenting their internal divisions, in a word, procuring their annihilation. Is this the way to proceed toward civilization?"[25] While Bilbao faulted the Chilean state for not doing enough to civilize the Mapuche, neither did he give them credit for their actions. He believed that trade had done much to modernize the Mapuche, particularly during periods of peace. Yet he also advocated that any gains in trade needed to be for the Chilean state, not the Mapuche. Furthermore, it was in Araucanía where the Chilean state's commercial transactions stood to gain the highest profits and benefits for the state, where "the rivers and the lakes invoke ships, the plains the railway, the mountains and her forests Christianity's ax, present[ed] all the necessary conditions for the establishment of great communities."[26]

In *Los Araucanos*, Bilbao questions how the Chilean state should address the Mapuche problem. For him there are two options: destruction or renewal. Not a proponent of Mapuche destruction (like Vicuña Mackenna), Bilbao instead advocates for the state to renew (*renovar*) Mapuches through positive incentives that include modeling appropriate behavior and communication. This way Mapuches could "preserve feelings toward the homeland, embracing their love for the new homeland whose name is synonymous with equality, they will keep the freedom of conscientiousness that has immortalized us but will renounce their hate at seeing that we are not men of the old tradition; they will renounce orgies, polygamy, superstition, and will contemplate solitary pride in their place."[27] Bilbao's vision of communication proposes to eradicate the abuses of certain behaviors, including the taking of indigenous lands, trade in alcohol such as aguardiente, and breeding discord among different indigenous groups. He believes the Chilean state needs to model the behavior it expects from the Mapuche rather than continue the Spanish model that had failed to produce results. The state should construct roads and railroads to facilitate greater trade, construct towns and cities to house the Mapuche, and provide them with civilization. As one historian points out, Bilbao was a liberal whose ideas ran counter to the autonomy and independence of all Mapuches: "The freedom and sovereignty of the indigenous societies and their territories are not recognized. Earlier or later, these territories will need to be integrated into the Republic and the Indians themselves will have to submit to the laws, that is to say, will need to become incorporated in civilization."[28] Thus, despite Bilbao's criticism of the Chilean government and its methods, he nonetheless affirms that the Mapuche's best interests lie in acquiescing to state demands on their lands and ways of life, guaranteeing a better life in a town, education, and better commerce—in short, a civilized life.

Both conservatives and liberals firmly believed that Chile needed to consolidate its national boundaries to build a modern, homogeneous society. And they believed that because Mapuches belonged to an inferior race that was impossible or very difficult to civilize, Mapuche lands in effect belonged to the state because it was the arbiter of a superior, white, European civilized society. For these intellectuals and government representatives, modernization or "development" meant Mapuche submission to the state, either by "reason or by force." One historian argues that this policy surpassed that of the colonial idea that Indians, because they were considered minors under Spanish law, needed to be protected through the mechanisms of evangelization and the *pueblos de indios* (Indian communities). Under this schema, Mapuches had two options: submit or cease to exist.[29] Although perhaps with a subtle difference in interpretation, the Chilean state, since its creation in the early nineteenth century, pursued policies toward Mapuches that were a *continuation* of the Spanish colonial state's goals of indigenous subjugation to European society and conversion to Christianity through evangelization. The Spanish crown's attempts at evangelization were mixed, as the example of the Colegio de Chillán mentioned in chapter 4 demonstrates. After independence, Chilean elites continued to believe that Mapuches were uncivilized and that subjugation was a primary goal.

Chilean intellectuals' racist views of the Mapuche had their counterpart in other parts of the world. Robert F. Berkhofer Jr., writing on racism toward indigenous peoples in the United States, contends that American individualism and liberalism were in direct opposition to what was considered Indian tribalism and tribal culture. Thus "Indians must join American society as individuals in the liberal state and economy rather than as tribes. Cultural assimilation, likewise, must proceed according to the values of individualism and not those of tribalism."[30] In another example, Berkhofer cites US congressional debates on the annexation of all Mexico after the US–Mexican war in 1848. "Many [congressmen] opposed the wholesale absorption of a population said to be biologically Indian on the grounds of the danger these people posed to American institutions."[31] Even though most politicians stressed the need to transform Indians and incorporate them into American society, few advocated miscegenation as a method to achieve that particular goal.[32]

Travelers' Writings on the Mapuche

Foreign travelers who arrived in Chile in the nineteenth century also had specific views and ideas about what Chilean civilization was like and what it should be. Foreign travelers were important because many of them spent an extended time in Chile, and a few even became permanent citizens and members of the elite class. The writings of travelers such as the English soldier Thomas Sutcliffe, the German naturalist Eduard Poeppig, and the Polish mineralogist and chemist Ignacio Domeyko, although problematic, also provide a window into the minds of what many elite Chileans believed an ideal society encompassed. These three men, as outsiders, had similar yet conflicting views of the Mapuche and their place in Chilean society.

Thomas Sutcliffe participated in the independence wars in Colombia in 1817. After spending time in jail in Cuba, he returned to England for a short period. In 1821, as a lieutenant, he sailed to Chile and stayed for the next sixteen years. There he worked with the newly formed Chilean state to liberate Peru, and eventually he became governor of San Juan Fernandez island (a Chilean penitentiary). In his *Sixteen Years in Chile and Peru: 1822–1839*, Sutcliffe details his military contributions to the young Chilean Republic and makes observations of different regions, including areas outside of Santiago and the city of Concepción. In the preface he relates, "I have ventured to write the following work, presenting my readers with a narrative of sixteen years' residence in South America; in the course of which I have described, in detail, *the manners and customs of the natives of Chile*; their struggle for independence, and the unfortunate political convulsions which have occurred, since their final emancipation from Spain, up to the period of the establishment of the government now in authority."[33] Suttcliffe's use of the term *natives* is noteworthy because he is not speaking about Mapuches but rather about Chilean creoles. In the few instances when he mentions Mapuches in his memoir, the language is partisan and ethnocentric, typical of European travelers to South America during this period.

Eduard Poeppig spent three years (1826–1829) in Chile, where he traveled to the north and south to explore and observe the flora and the fauna of the country. According to his translator, Poeppig "fully captured Chile. Although he always maintained the objectivity and the composure of a scientist, there is not a single line in his work that does not sympathize with the Chilean."[34] Poeppig himself writes, "A Chilean, without excluding those from the lower classes, never behaves irrationally or rudely, and with an insatiable curiosity, will always find an ingenious pretext to visit a foreigner with a distinguished pedigree."[35] For proof of a Chilean's outgoing and friendly demeanor to foreigners, Poeppig refers to the "more than 3,000 Spaniards [who] remained in Chile after the revolution, who were never persecuted and are now regarded with the same respect as native born sons."[36]

The same friendliness and mutual respect did not extend to the Mapuche communities Poeppig visited and observed throughout his travels in

Chile's south. He was far less enthusiastic about their ability to coexist with Chileans in this modernized, post-revolutionary world. On his observations of the Pehuenches and their work practices, he writes, "The productive work of the adults has little importance, limiting itself, in general to the making of objects which they consider indispensable to satisfy their vanity and their mania with adorning themselves. Even when some of them work with metals, which they get in brute form from the Chileans, the products they create are very coarse, and thus the hammers are replaced with sharp rocks."[37]

Poeppig's description clearly insinuates that the Pehuenches' work style was basic and premodern, and therefore unproductive. In another example, Poeppig travels to a fort in Trubunleo, where he witnesses the execution of two Pehuenche prisoners of an enemy Pehuenche group. His main complaint related to the lack of a confession on behalf of those "wretches . . . who perhaps had nothing to confess," and he intervened, claiming that "humanity required that they be set free."[38] The prisoners remained under guard, to be sent to Los Angeles the next day, but they escaped. One prisoner fell off a precipice to his death, and the other was killed while fleeing.[39] Not only did the "wretches" never confess, but Poeppig's intrusion on behalf of what *he* perceived to be justice brought these prisoners to possibly a worse death. Poeppig's meddling reflected his disdain for Mapuche methods of justice within their own jurisdictions and against their own members.

In 1838 Ignacio Domeyko accepted an invitation from the Chilean government to teach chemistry and minerology at a school in Coquimbo. For the next several years, Domeyko traveled within Chile and other countries. In Chile's north, he confronted serious deforestation because of Chile's growing dependence on mineral extraction and the use of wood as fuel. Domeyko also traveled extensively throughout Araucanía, writing about its beauty as well as describing the complexity of the relationship between the Mapuche and their lands. In 1846 he published *Araucanía y sus habitantes: recuerdo de un viaje hecho en las provincias meridionales de Chile, en los meses de enero y febrero de 1845*. His justification for writing this volume reflected on his observations that Chileans loved their country and how quickly Chile had progressed with respect to order and civilization. Nonetheless, Domeyko found it strange that Chile, being a "free and sovereign nation," still had "savages who are strangers to the divine light of Christianity" living within its borders. To integrate them,

Chileans would need to "*first*, study the physical and natural habitat of the country that the Mapuche inhabit: *second*, study their actual moral standing and their customs; and *third*, study the causes for why such Indians are opposed to civilization, and find the most opportune solutions that Chile should pursue in having them submit."[40] His tone is contradictory throughout the work, particularly the section on the moral character of Mapuches, where he tends to severely criticize while simultaneously admiring them. For example, he describes how Indians are "generally mean, lazy, and have a propensity for drunkenness."[41] Yet he also claims, in the same section, that "there is no doubt that the Indian *knows* what is just and unjust, the difference between probity and malice, generosity and baseness, just like any other human provided with a heart and soul."[42] For Domeyko, Mapuches act differently depending on whether they are at war or not. In times of peace, he attributes their behavior to being essentially the same as a civilized European: "Upon seeing him in this state [of peace], any traveler who limits himself to observing the interior character of the Chilean Indian . . . will not take him for being a barbarian: on the contrary, he will consider him to have the same advantages as any Christian community."[43]

Domeyko's observations of the Mapuche community were, like those of Thomas Sutcliffe, Eduard Poeppig, and so many others of the nineteenth century, tainted with his own notions of what constituted a civilized and orderly society. As a European he believed that civility and good community derived from the European model, a model he grappled with in his own observations of people he perceived as inferior and barbaric, even before observing them. He visited Araucanía to provide the Chilean state with a viable way to integrate Mapuches or to "reduce" them, which was more expedient. His writings, however, demonstrate a much more conflicted and complicated picture of Mapuches, and perhaps one that Domeyko himself did not expect to find during his travels in Araucanía. The Mapuche were "at peace" in 1845, when he visited. His preconceived racist views of them did not fully reflect his actual experiences, and his writings illustrate that ambiguity.

Like so many other foreigners and noteworthy Chilean intellectuals in this period, Domeyko represents the complicated nature of how ideologies, whether liberal or conservative, colored how people "observed" each other throughout the nineteenth century. These observations were significant because the Chilean state formulated policy based on many of these people's writings, all of which were ultimately detrimental to Mapuche communities themselves.

The Mapuche

What about the Mapuche themselves? What was Mapuche society like post-independence? How integrated were they in the first half of the nineteenth century, and why did Mapuche integration into the larger Chilean society matter with respect to citizenship?

First and foremost, Mapuche society by the early nineteenth century was complex and very much integrated into the Chilean Republic, expressed best in the economy. The Mapuche had a very advanced cattle trading system, originally established during the colonial period and expanded during the early nineteenth century. Araucanía was also home to an army with a diverse membership that at one point had fewer than seven hundred soldiers. Frontier society was complex. Capitanes de amigos, oftentimes army representatives to the various parlamentos held throughout the colonial period and continued throughout the early nineteenth century, also served as lenguaraces (translators) at these meetings. Frontier towns also had *comisarios de naciones*, who acted as the civil authority. *Tenientes* were like the capitanes de amigos but served in a more local capacity. Lastly, caciques played a major role in maintaining peace and order on the frontier. Many of them received a salary for their endeavors.

There was a period of relative peace in Araucanía between 1825 and 1867, but essentially two separate societies coexisted. Although cattle ranching remained the primary economic activity, Mapuches tended to live in their own communities with their own customs. Many adopted outward appearances of Chilean sociability through their choice of dress and other European articles, learning the Spanish language and even converting to Catholicism.[44] The vast majority of Mapuche indigenous groups during this period, however, were territorially and politically independent from the Chilean Republic. Much to Bilbao's chagrin, I am sure, Mapuches refused to live in towns (*pueblos*) and did not care for monogamy, which is why, although they adopted aspects of Christianity, if monogamy became a precondition for full conversion, many Mapuches

abandoned Christianity entirely. It is precisely because Mapuches were independent—that is, they owned their territory and politically and economically
managed their own affairs—that they were willing to adopt some Chilean
cultural norms and sometimes perhaps look and act Chilean. Mapuches, then,
never fully integrated into the dominant European model of Chilean society,
and once the Chilean state began to systematically take away Mapuche territory (either spontaneously, illegally, or legally), because Mapuches believed
themselves to be an independent nation-state, they fought back to protect what
was, in their view, rightfully their territory. To some extent, civilization or
integration into Chilean society, for Mapuches at least, was neither a priority
nor a necessity.

Since at least independence, spontaneous Chilean colonization existed
in Araucanía, and it usually took two forms: informal land purchases at
below-market prices from caciques willing to sell, and legal purchases
through legislation the Chilean state passed in 1866. Spontaneous coloniz-
ers, who purchased as few as five hundred *cuadras* (one cuadra is roughly
equivalent to eighty by eighty meters) to more than one thousand cuadras,
often purchased them at very low prices. The nature of the transactions
made it difficult for the Chilean state to administer the newly acquired
lands. To remedy this situation, in December 1866 the state passed a law
whereby parcels bought extralegally became state property, as it says in
article 1, "Found [parcels of land] ... in indigenous territory that the President of the Republic designates. The State should acquire all particular
property that is deemed convenient for this and other goals of the present
law."[45] The law also required that, in addition to acquiring "appropriate"
property, the state populate the newly acquired lands. This law coincided
with a period of European immigration to Araucanía, particularly from
Germany. These European immigrants were encouraged to settle in areas
in "indigenous territorial sites, that the President of the Republic desig-
nate, that the State should acquire those territories and particular properties
that may be convenient for it and for the rest of the objects of the present
law."[46]

A newspaper article in *El Meteoro de Los Angeles* on December 15, 1866,
mentioned how the state should tread carefully in dealing with indigenous
belongings and should be prudent in administering justice. Doing otherwise
was an invitation to war with the Indian population. The same article

continues, "One should not introduce too many violent innovations because the Indians are not yet able to submit to a constitutional system."[47] With these cautionary moves, the state believed that civilizing Indians would be manageable.

As the heated debates in congress in 1868 demonstrated, however, civilizing and integrating Mapuches was not easily accomplished. Cornelio Saavedra's frontier policy lasted six relatively peaceful years, 1861 to 1867. More violence, death, and destruction came later. In total, the Chilean state's conquest, occupation, and "pacification" of Araucanía took twenty-four years to complete (1859–1883),[48] and the clear majority of these years inflicted devastation and death on the Mapuche communities affected.

After 1881, the state implemented various strategies to incorporate the Mapuche into Chilean society, including the continuation of employing and paying salaries to local caciques, who in turn had the power to allocate lands and establish local authority, and maintaining indigenous autonomy.[49] Unfortunately, private interests wanting cheap and fertile lands, coupled with increased pressure to push the Mapuche to lands toward the ocean or the mountains, exacerbated the already tenuous relationship between local caciques, their communities, and the state.

Conclusion

In the middle of the nineteenth century, the Chilean Republic's leaders pursued a state-building project that included the acquisition of all lands south of the Bío-Bío River either by "reason or by force" to build roads, railroads, towns, and schools and to expand agricultural production for export. An aggressive policy that encouraged Europeans to immigrate to this region provided the labor required to modernize Chile's economy while simultaneously maintaining an advanced society. In the state's view—reflected by elite intellectuals such as Diego Barros Arana, Francisco Bilbao, and Benjamín Vicuña Mackenna, as well as by European travelers such as Thomas Sutcliffe, Eduard Poeppig, and Ignacio Domeyko—the Mapuche's integration into this society required their complete submission to state demands for their lands and culture. For Mapuches, who had maintained their independence from state encroachment since the colonial period, subjugation within a country (nation-state) they did not recognize meant nothing. Consequently, rather than adapt to Chilean society, the Mapuche became second-class citizens within their own territorial boundaries.

CHAPTER SEVEN

Concluding Thoughts

The Mapuche fight for their land, their liberty, their women, their children, and their pursuit of happiness, which for them means never being conquered ... and never governed by the King [of Spain], nor by a foreign power. This is how Ercilla saw it and handed it down to us in the verses of *La Araucana*.

—RICARDO FERRANDO KEUN[1]

STATE FORMATION IN POST-INDEPENDENCE LATIN AMERICA WAS A chaotic, violent, and uneven process, with most of the newly liberated countries struggling to conform to new republican models of government while also maintaining privileges in place since the early days of Spanish (and Portuguese) colonization. Indians played an important role in these upheavals, and their participation differed depending on their status prior to independence and their involvement in the independence wars, whether as royalists loyal to the Spanish crown or as supporters of the Spanish-creole patriots. Moreover, as David Weber has demonstrated, whether or not Indians then became active participants in the newly independent republics was contingent upon their colonial relationships to said parties, a contention I argue throughout this book with respect to the Mapuche of Chile.[2] Despite the chaos of the 1820s, Chilean leaders instituted a strong, centralized state, and with the 1833 constitution they succeeded in establishing an institutional framework that provided a legal forum to solve political disputes between the country's liberals and conservatives through a power-sharing arrangement with the trappings of popular democratic participation. The Chilean system, like many others in Latin America in the first half of the nineteenth century, passed literacy and property requirements for voting, limiting suffrage and disenfranchising most of the population, including the Mapuche.

Chile's leaders (whether liberal or conservative) also shared the common goals of territorial acquisition beyond the existing southern border, as well as subjugation of the region's Mapuche inhabitants. Prior to 1833, this goal proved elusive as the state battled against holdout Spanish generals and their Mapuche and bandit allies. Chile's leaders also fought among themselves during the civil war of 1829–1830. At least through the 1820s, then, Chile's state looked very much like other countries newly liberated from Spain. Notably, however, during this period those who professed royalism were a diverse group that included Mapuches and bandits, and they did so under the pretext of protecting longheld alliances with the Spanish crown that allowed them a significant amount of autonomy to conduct their own affairs politically, economically, and socially.

The institution of parlamentos, held between Spanish authorities and the Mapuche during the colonial period, served as a testament of the power and influence Mapuches held in the borderlands of Araucanía. The continuation of these parlamentos well into the nineteenth century attests to the importance the Chilean state placed on these treaty negotiations, even when it no longer considered the Mapuche communities an independent nation-state but rather a subjugated group. Creole leaders adopted and formalized native indigenous practices to achieve their own goals of state expansion and conquest.

Nonetheless, at no period, whether colonial or post-independence, did either the Spanish crown or the Chilean state consider Mapuches legitimate citizens. Fundamentally, both under the Spanish Empire and under the newly created Chilean Republic, Mapuches were subjects to be molded into the larger empirical and liberal as well as conservative model of what was a legitimate, and thus a civilized, society. That society was European and Christian. So the crown established missions in Araucanía and educated the sons of caciques at the Colegio Propaganda Fide. These policies continued after the independence upheavals, when the Chilean state reopened the school. Mapuches themselves were not necessarily swayed by these policies.

Many caciques educated at the Colegio Propaganda Fide retained, ironically, their allegiance to the Spanish crown throughout the independence wars, which allowed groups such as the Chillán Pehuenches and their Pincheira allies to maintain their territorial and economic autonomy throughout the tumultuous decade of the 1820s. Additionally, significant changes within the leadership characteristics of the different Mapuche groups weakened traditional political and economic relationships in Araucanía. The centralization of political power at the top echelons of Mapuche society further fragmented historically unstable alliances within and across the various Mapuche groups.

The Pincheira Legacy

After his surrender on March 11, 1832, José Antonio Pincheira retired to Quilúa, a small property he had inherited from his father in the district of San Fabián de Alico, Department of San Carlos. José Antonio "never again involved himself in any type of politics, preferring instead to live a quiet and peaceful life."[3] He died in 1884, but his legacy as a bandit to some and a hero to others lived on in Chilean popular culture. Zig-Zag Press published *Los Pincheira* in the 1930s with the following foreword: "Magdalena Petit has conquered a prominent place in Chilean literature with her novels and biographies, in which history plays a fundamental role, but that also infuse the reader with a sense of adventure. . . . Among all her books, perhaps the most popular and attractive would be *Los Pincheira*."[4] In the prologue, Petit mentions how her curiosity about the Pincheiras inspired her to write the novel and "the curiosity that existed among the general public in wanting to know more about these celebrated montoneros, of whom only a scarce number of historical facts and brief stories from travelers are known."[5] Although the main character in *Los Pincheira* is a young woman the Pincheiras captured, Petit portrays them as strong men willing to fight for their beliefs. First printed in 1930, *Los Pincheira* was so successful that a second edition was printed in 1949.

The Pincheira brothers are cultural icons in modern Chile.[6] Their *malal* (camp) high up in the Andes cordillera is a cave where modern tourists can watch actors, clad in black and on horseback, reenact many of the Pincheira brothers' various exploits and listen to their stories. One tourist website states,

"In addition to telling the world about their adventures, the staging includes on-horse skills and blank shooting which amaze visitors. The natural environment of the cave and the historical representation justify a halt in the tour to see this amusing attraction at Las Trancas Valley."[7] The Pincheira name is still prominent in the area, and *Los Pincheira*, a *telenovela* (soap opera), debuted in 2004 on Chile's TVN to some critical acclaim. It was the story of three brothers at the beginning of the twentieth century. With the recruitment of a fourth member who was looking for revenge against a landowner's treatment of his father, the four turned to banditry. A love triangle between two of the brothers and a prominent woman also provided drama.

The story of the Pincheira brothers and their Pehuenche allies, as well as other Mapuche stories described in *Contested Nation: The Mapuche, Bandits, and State Formation in Nineteenth-Century Chile* adds another element to the growing borderlands historiography of Latin America. Araucanía was simultaneously a border, a frontier, and a separate nation-state. The economic interactions, along with the concurrent violence and parlamentos between the Spanish and the Mapuche, shaped Araucanía and made the region integral to the late colonial empire. With Chilean independence, Araucanía as a border/frontier and separate nation-state became crucial to the territorial integrity of the new Chilean Republic. As the nineteenth century progressed, Chile's leaders first eliminated their Spanish enemies and their bandit and Mapuche allies. They then took advantage of a changed indigenous political landscape to skillfully navigate fractured Mapuche relations and press their advantage in the region. Utilizing indigenous methods such as the parlamentos, enticements backed up by force, and superior resources, Chilean leaders systemically proceeded to erase the Araucanian border and subsume Araucanía itself into the new territorial boundaries of the Chilean Republic. Araucanía, then, played a critical role in the establishment of a stable political and economic state in Chile in the nineteenth century. As a consequence, the Mapuche became disenfranchised second-class citizens in a republic they at once did not recognize as such and could not opt out of. Thus the Mapuche fought for their "land, their liberty, their women, and their children."[8] They also defended and protected their political, economic, and social independence within their territory until the end of the nineteenth century, when Ercilla's *La Araucana*,[9] unfortunately, ceased to exist for the Mapuche of Araucanía.

APPENDIX

Parlamentos *1825 and After*

Document Title	Date	Location
Parlamento General de Tapihue[1]	January 7, 1825	Tapihue
El Tratado de Tantauco[2]	January 19, 1826	Tantauco
Parlamento de Boroa	1837	Boroa
Junta General de Tucapel[3]	March 4, 1860	Tucapel
Parlamento con Cornelio Saavedra[4]	July 15, 1867	Ángol
La Paz celebrada con los Araucanos[5]	September 25, 1869	Ipinco
Parlamento de Toltén[6]	January 22, 1870	Toltén
Tratado de Paz entre el Coronel José Francisco Gana, Intendente de la Provincia de Arauco y El Cacique Quilahueque en Representación de los Indios Arribanos[7]	July 5, 1871	Arauco
Convenio entre el Gobierno de Chile y los Pehuenches	January 1, 1872	Ángol
Tratado de Paz	July 5, 1876	Collipulli

1. León, *O'Higgins*; Painemal, *Los Tratados*, 293–97; Téllez L. et al., "El Tratado."
2. Painemal, *Los Tratados*, 298–300.
3. Mauricio Barbosa to minister of war, March 4, 1860, vol. 457, Archivo Ministerio de la Guerra.
4. Bengoa, *Historia Del Pueblo Mapuche*, 197.
5. Painemal, *Los Tratados*, 189–90. Original document in vol. 13, 1870–1877, Archivo Histórico de Propaganda Fide (Roma) Sc. América Meridional.
6. Saavedra, *Documentos relativos*, 207–08.
7. Painemal, *Los Tratados*, 308–9.

NOTES

Chapter One

1. *El Araucano*, January 28, 1832, 3.
2. Bolívar, *Selected Writings*, 11.
3. Araucanía was the name of the territory between the Bío-Bío and Toltén Rivers in Chile's south.
4. *Pacification* is the term the Chilean state officially utilized in its documentation, a term that certainly implies domination and taking away rights from the Mapuche. The reality for the Mapuche became total subjugation of a "pacified" population.
5. In a series of articles, Guillaume Boccara (Boccara, "Notas"; Boccara, "Etnogénesis Mapuche") suggests the term *Mapuche* rather than *Araucanian*, which he considers to be ethnocentric.
6. Boccara, "Notas"; Boccara, "Etnogénesis Mapuche."
7. Jones, "Warfare, Reorganization, and Readaptation."
8. Jones, 143.
9. Boccara, "Notas," 660n2.
10. Boccara, "Notas."
11. Bengoa, *Historia Del Pueblo Mapuche*, 68.
12. Boccara, "Notas."
13. Bengoa, *Historia Del Pueblo* Mapuche, 66.
14. Warren, "A Nation Divided."
15. Boccara, "Políticas indígenas en Chile."
16. Poeppig, *Un testigo*, 386–87.
17. Boccara, "Notas," 671.
18. Poeppig, 387.
19. León Solis, *Maloqueros y Conchavadores*.
20. Collier and Sater, *A History of Chile*, 38.
21. Ferrando Keun, *Y Así Nació La Frontera*, 293.
22. Ferrando Keun, 293.
23. Ferrando Keun, 293.

24. Bengoa, *Historia Del Pueblo Mapuche*, 142.

25. Loveman, *Chile*, 120.

26. Echeverri, *Indian and Slave Royalists*.

27. Turner, *Early Writings*.

28. Guy and Sheridan, *Contested Ground*, 10.

29. Weber, *Spanish Frontier*, 11.

30. White, *Middle Ground*.

31. Adelman and Aron, "From Borderlands to Borders"; Wunder and Hämäläinen, "Of Lethal Places."

32. For examples, see DuVal, *Native Ground*; DeLay, *War of a Thousand Deserts*; Hämäläinen, *Comanche Empire*; León, *O'Higgins*; León Solis, *La Araucanía*.

33. Hobsbawm, *Bandits*, 18.

34. Slatta, *Bandidos*; Taylor, "Banditry and Insurrection"; Aguirre et al., *Bandoleros*, 90; Contador, *Los Pincheira*.

35. Daitsman, "Bandolerismo."

36. Daitsman, 264.

37. Slatta, *Bandidos*; Taylor, "Banditry and Insurrection"; Aguirre et al., *Bandoleros*.

38. Lewin, "Oligarchical Limitations."

39. Taylor, "Banditry and Insurrection"; Vanderwood, "Nineteenth-Century Mexico's Profiteering Bandits."

40. Taylor, "Banditry and Insurrection," 207.

41. Taylor, 207.

42. Vanderwood, "Nineteenth-Century Mexico's Profiteering Bandits," 67.

43. Walker, "Montoneros, bandoleros, malhechores," 108.

44. Joseph, "On the Trail," 108.

45. Joseph, 19.

46. Dabove, *Bandit Narratives*, 253.

47. Dabove, 267.

48. Frazer, *Bandit Nation*, 2.

49. Frazer, 12.

50. Chambers, *Families in War and Peace*, 15.

51. See Mariluán's case in chapter 4.

Chapter Two

1. Loveman, *Constitution of Tyranny*, 31.

2. Valencia Avaria, *Anales de La República*, 68–69.

3. Valencia Avaria, 71.

4. Valencia Avaria, 73.

5. Valencia Avaria, 65; Loveman, *Constitution of Tyranny*, 320.

6. Valencia Avaria, 65; Loveman, 320.

7. Loveman, 323.

8. Loveman, 323.

9. Benjamín Vicuña Mackenna, March 3, 1819, vol. 42, fol. 3, Archivo Vicuña Mackenna. Sarah Chambers's *Families in War and Peace* has an excellent discussion of this period and the conflicts over pardoning ex-royalists.

10. Loveman, *Chile*, 118.

11. Collier and Sater, *History of Chile*, 48.

12. Valencia Avaria, *Anales de La República*, 145; Loveman, *Constitution of Tyranny*, 324.

13. Valencia Avaria, 145.

14. Loveman, *Constitution of Tyranny*, 325.

15. Loveman, *Chile*, 120.

16. Encina and Castedo, *Resumen*, 779.

17. Encina and Castedo, 779.

18. Villalobos R., *Portales*, 79.

19. Loveman, *Constitution of Tyranny*, 329.

20. Valencia Avaria, *Anales de La República*, 117.

21. Valencia Avaria, 154.

22. Wood, *Society of Equality*, 62.

23. Wood, 69.

24. Encina and Castedo, *Resumen*, 814–15.

25. Encina and Castedo, 816–17.

26. Vice consul of Valparaiso, December 14, 1829, fol. 16, reel 4, vols. 8–10, British Foreign Office, General Correspondence, Chile, Indiana University Library.

27. Wood, *Society of Equality*, 69.

28. Vice consul of Valparaiso, December 14, 1829, fol. 16, reel 4, vols. 8–10, British Foreign Office, General Correspondence, Chile, Indiana University Library.

29. Vice consul of Valparaiso.

30. Portales et al., *Epistolario*, 58.

31. Loveman, *Constitution of Tyranny*, 335; Portales et al., *Epistolario*, 58.

32. Wood, *Society of Equals*, 45.

33. Wood, 45.

34. *El Araucano*, March 24, 1832, sec. 80.

35. Loveman, *Constitution of Tyranny*, 330.

36. Bauer, *Chilean Rural Society*, 64.

37. Pérez Rosales and Mellafe R., *Ensayo sobre Chile*, 235.

38. Pérez Rosales and Mellafe R., 235.

39. Pérez Rosales and Mellafe R., 247.

40. Pérez Rosales and Mellafe R., 237.

41. Pérez Rosales and Mellafe R., 250.

42. Góngora, *Origen*, 63, 103; Bauer, *Chilean Rural Society*, 146.

43. Bauer, *Chilean Rural* Society, 146.

44. Salazar Vergara, *Labradores*, 117.

45. Salazar Vergara, 177.

46. Salazar Vergara, 177.

47. Salazar Vergara, 178.

48. Salazar Vergara, 178.

49. Vicuña Mackenna, *La guerra a muerte*, 289.

50. Vicuña Mackenna, 295.

51. Vicuña Mackenna, 287–95.

52. Vicuña Mackenna, 283–94.

53. Luis Salazar, "Mes de Enero 1824," January 27, 1824, vol. 75, Archivo Intendencia de Concepción.

54. Pedro Barnachea, "Mes de Enero 1824," January 27, 1824, vol. 75, Archivo Intendencia de Concepción.

55. Pedro Barnachea, "Mes de Julio 1824," July 8, 1824, vol. 75, no. 531, Archivo Intendencia de Concepción.

56. Vicuña Mackenna, *La guerra a muerte*, 230–34; Campos Harriet, *Los defensores*, 237–63.

57. Vicente Benavides to don Agustin Elisondo, December 17, 1819, vol. 42, fols. 196–202, Archivo Vicuña Mackenna.

58. Vicuña Mackenna, *La guerra a muerte*, 574–87.

59. Pedro Barnachea, "Mes de octubre," October 31, 1824, vol. 75, Archivo Intendencia de Concepción. See Campos Harriet, *Los defensores del rey*.

60. Some of these celebrated royalists included the Catholic priest Ferrebú and Don Antonio de Quintanilla y Santiago. See Campos Harriet, *Los defensores del rey*.

61. Beauchef, *Memorias Militares*, 255.

62. Barnachea, "Mes de octubre," 258.

63. Barnachea, 265.

64. Letter by José Antonio Pincheira, February 10, 1827, quoted in Beauchef, *Memorias*, 266.

65. Beauchef, 258.

66. Beauchef, 265.

67. *El Verdadero Liberal*, March 27, 1827, 107. The same newspaper had published another of Beauchef's "victory" letters a month earlier. The following is an excerpt: "It would not be surprising if this bandit, seeing us approaching, would try to surrender. He has no escape if the general can put in movement, which I have no doubts that he can, the other two divisions that are identical to his, 230 men under his command, this not including the Indians that should be added: the two squadrons are very good, with 240 strong. With this many, there are more than enough for Pincheira. Besides, the Indians wait for us with many hopes." *El Verdadero Liberal*, February 2, 1827, 28.

68. Beauchef, *Memorias Militares*, 275.

69. *El Verdadero Liberal*, July 3, 1827, 2.

70. *El Verdadero Liberal*, March 27, 1827, 107.

71. On many occasions, Pincheira used his influence to disrupt trade among the different Mapuche groups or would outright raid their towns and take away their women if they did not support his activities in the area. The following excerpt from a letter by Pedro Barnachea, commander of the frontier, to his superior in the summer of 1823 provides an example of Pincheira's powerful influence. Barnachea writes: "Said captains bring four messengers from the principal caciques with them: Millanao, Llancamilla, Talcuaman and Chorinquillan, with the object of sending a representative to their lands to sign an agreement . . . *they also say they do not want to have anything to do with Pincheira anymore, that because of him their trade has faltered* [emphasis mine]." December 13, 1823, vol. 51, no. 80, Archivo Intendencia de Concepción.

72. Beauchef, *Memorias*, 258.

73. Beauchef, 258.

74. *Rol del Policía*, April 28, 1827, sec. 1.

75. Loveman, *Chile*; Loveman, *Constitution of Tyranny*; Collier and Sater, *History of Chile*; Villalobos R., *Portales*; Woll, *Functional Past*.

76. Loveman, *Constitution of Tyranny*, 329.

77. Loveman, *Chile*, 124.

78. Portales, *Diego Portales*, 10.

79. Villalobos R., *Portales*, 10.

80. Bernardo Bravo Lira, "Portales entre dos Constituciones," *El Mercurio*, June 11, 1995.

81. Bravo Lira.

82. Bravo Lira.

83. *El Araucano*, April 24, 1831, no. 84, sec. 2.

84. Portales, *Diego Portales*, 58; Portales et al., *Epistolario*, 190.

85. Portales, 58; Portales et al., 190.

86. Portales, 58.

87. Collier and Sater, *History of Chile*, 54.

88. Loveman, *Constitution of Tyranny*, 331; Valencia Avaria, *Anales de La República*, 176, 182.

89. Valencia Avaria, *Anales de La República*, 185.

90. Valencia Avaria, 180; Loveman, *Constitution of Tyranny*, 331.

91. Valencia Avaria, 186.

92. Loveman, *Constitution of Tyranny*, 8.

93. Valencia Avaria, *Anales de La República*, 174.

94. Loveman, *Constitution of Tyranny*, 332.

95. Loveman, 332.

96. Loveman, 332; Villalobos R., *Portales*, 122.

Chapter Three

1. *El Monitor Imparcial*, March 14, 1828, sec. 28.
2. Vanderwood, "Nineteenth-Century Mexico's Profiteering Bandits," 65.
3. For a different interpretation of the Pincheira brothers and their bandit activities, see Contador, *Los Pincheira*.
4. Benjamín Vicuña Mackenna, vol. 42, fol. 28, Archivo Vicuña Mackenna.
5. Errázuriz, *Chile bajo el imperio*.
6. Vicuña Mackenna, *La guerra a muerte*, 494.
7. Vicuña Mackenna, 494.
8. See for examples, Vicuña Mackenna, vol. 24, fols. 9–10, 13, 100–103, Archivo Vicuña Mackenna; *El Araucano*, January 21, 1832, 1; Vicuña Mackenna, *La guerra a muerte*, 742n.
9. In her novelized biography, *Los Pincheira*, Magdalena Petit describes José Antonio's character: "because his peaceful character certainly did not fit in with the requirements of the profession of a guerrilla, and neither did the title of banditry fit him now that the raids began taking on a different character since the excuse of defending the King of Spain was no longer working," 178.
10. It is not clear exactly when José Antonio's leadership began and his brother Pablo's ended. The documents frequently cite "Pincheira" or "Pincheyra" but rarely identify the exact brother. José Antonio wrote two of the four existing Pincheira letters. See August 9, 1820, vol. 20, Archivo Intendencia de Concepción, and letter in Beauchef and Feliú Cruz, *Memorias Militares*.
11. Feliú Cruz, *Conversaciones*, 130.
12. Vicuña Mackenna, *La guerra a muerte*, 494.
13. "Oficio del governador intendente de concepcion," *Gobierno Intendente*, December 3, 1825, 2.
14. *El Valdiviano Federal*, February 13, 1827.
15. Bengoa, *Historia del Pueblo Mapuche*, 144.
16. Bengoa, 144.
17. Barros Arana, *Historia Jeneral de Chile*, XVI:114–15.
18. Barros Arana, 115.
19. Feliú Cruz, *Conversaciones*, 131.
20. April 30, 1819, vol. 20, Archivo Intendencia de Concepción, San Carlos.
21. William Henry Rouse, December 30, 1829, fol. 16, reel 5, vols. 11–12A, British Foreign Office, General Correspondence, Chile, Indiana University Library.
22. May 20, 1820, vol. 20, Archivo Intendencia de Concepción, San Carlos.
23. April 9, 1824, vol. 75, Archivo Intendencia de Concepción, Yumbel.
24. Errázuriz, *Chile bajo el imperio*, 54.
25. Errázuriz, 54.
26. December 18, 1823, vol. 51, no. 88, 14–19, Archivo Intendencia de Concepción.
27. November 15, 1823, vol. 51, Archivo Intendencia de Concepción.
28. December 18, 1823, vol. 51, no. 88, Archivo Intendencia de Concepción.

29. November 23, 1823, vol. 51, no. 80, Archivo Intendencia de Concepción.

30. November 18, 1823, vol. 51, Archivo Intendencia de Concepción.

31. December 10, 1823, vol. 51, Archivo Intendencia de Concepción.

32. March 5, 1824, vol. 75. Archivo Intendencia de Concepción. See vols. 51 and 75, for other examples.

33. December 23, 1823, vol. 51, no. 80, Archivo Intendencia de Concepción.

34. From the trial of José María Bentancur, accused of being one of the Pincheiras' spies: "Don Jacinto Albarez of Lffongaví [a local hacendado] was sending four bushels of flour and four of wheat and . . . wanted to let Pincheyra know that he would send anything else he may wish: and to also let him know that don Ramóyn Freyre had fared well in Chiloé, that they had taken it for the *Patria*." Judicial de Concepción, February 28, 1826, file 74, Archivo Nacional de Chile.

35. Barros Arana, *Historia Jeneral de Chile*, II:270n3.

36. *El Verdadero Liberal*, April 20, 1827.

37. Judicial de Concepción, February 28, 1826, file 74, Archivo Nacional de Chile; Judicial de Concepción, April 20, 1831, file 156, Archivo Nacional de Chile; Judicial de San Felipe, 1831, file 69, Archivo Nacional de Chile.

38. Judicial de Concepción, February 28, 1826, file 74:3, Archivo Nacional de Chile.

39. "Criminal contra el espía de Pincheyra José María Bentacur," Judicial de Concepción, February 28, 1826, file 74, Archivo Nacional de Chile.

40. "Ciudad de San Felipe, año 1831, contra José María Concha por acusado de espía del bandido Pincheira—confesión y resumen," Judicial de San Felipe, 1831, file 69, Archivo Nacional de Chile.

41. "Ciudad de San Felipe, año 1831."

42. "Ciudad de San Felipe, año 1831, contra José María Concha por acusado de espía del bandido Pincheira—confesión de Cecilio Tofre," Judicial de San Felipe, 1831, file 69, Archivo Nacional de Chile.

43. *El Valdiviano Federal*, August 19, 1829, article 2.

44. *El Valdiviano Federal*, August 19, 1829, articles 3 and 4.

45. *El Valdiviano Federal*, August 19, 1829, article 5.

46. *El Valdiviano Federal*, August 19, 1829, article 5.

47. *El Araucano*, January 8, 1831.

48. *El Araucano*, January 8, 1831.

49. *El Araucano*, January 8, 1831.

50. Barros Arana, *Historia Jeneral de Chile*, XVI:98–99.

51. Barros Arana, 98–99.

52. Barros Arana, 98–99.

53. Barros Arana, 98.

54. Barros Arana, 98–99.

55. *Documentos Officiales*, January 16, 1832, no. 32, Archivo Nacional, Santiago Chile.

56. *El Araucano*, January 21, 1832, no. 71.

57. *El Araucano*, March 24, 1832, no. 80; Barros Arana, *Historia Jeneral de Chile*, XVI:111; Vicuña Mackenna, *La guerra a muerte*, 742n.

58. Valenzuela, "Bandidaje y guerrilla," 4.

59. Vicente Peres Rosales, ed., *Diego Barros Arana: Paginas escogidas, Semblanza de Diego Barros Arana* (Santiago: Editorial Universitaria, Biblioteca Nacional, 1987), 374. Emphasis mine.

60. Dawe, *Contesting Cosmologies*, 25. Also see Valenzuela Márquez, *Bandidaje*.

61. Dawe, 25.

62. Barros Arana, *Historia Jeneral de Chile*, XVI:98.

Chapter Four

1. Lázaro A., "Capítulo IX," 205.

2. Lázaro A., 208–9; emphasis mine.

3. Bengoa, *Historia Del Pueblo Mapuche*, 64.

4. Bengoa, 66.

5. Bengoa, 44.

6. Poeppig, *Un testigo*, 387.

7. Poeppig, 387.

8. Bengoa, *Historia Del Pueblo Mapuche*, 44.

9. Bengoa, 50.

10. Bengoa, 51.

11. Vol. 42, fols. 29–33, Archivo Vicuña Mackenna.

12. Bengoa, *Historia del Pueblo Mapuche*, 141–43.

13. For a more detailed explanation of these conflicts, see Herr, "The Nation-State According to Whom?"

14. Bengoa, 141.

15. Vicuña Mackenna, *La guerra a muerte*, 184.

16. Vicuña Mackenna, 620–21.

17. Vicuña Mackenna, 681.

18. *El Araucano*, January 28, 1832, 3.

19. *El Araucano*, January 28, 1832, 3.

20. *El Araucano*, January 28, 1832, 4.

21. See Petit, *Los Pincheira*, for a fictional example of what the Pehuenche–Pincheira montonera did with their captives.

22. Bengoa, *Historia Del Pueblo Mapuche*, 80n21.

23. Vicuña Mackenna, *La guerra a muerte*, 681.

24. Sutcliffe, *Sixteen Years*, 158.

25. Vicuña Mackenna, *La guerra a muerte*, 681.

26. Bengoa, *Historia Del Pueblo Mapuche*, 144.

27. Bengoa, 82.

28. Bengoa, 82.

29. Bengoa, 83.

30. Vicuña Mackenna, *La guerra a muerte*, 675, 680.

31. August 9, 1820, vol. 20, Archivo Intendencia de Concepción,

32. Pilguén, January 4, 1824, Archivo Intendencia de Concepción.

33. Pilguén, January 7, 1824, Archivo Intendencia de Concepción.

34. Vol. 75, no. 134, Archivo Intendencia de Concepción. See also Vicuña Mackenna, *La guerra a muerte*, 773.

35. Pilguén, vol. 75, March 5, 1824, Archivo Intendencia de Concepción.

36. Concepción, vol. 75, March 11, 1824, Archivo Intendencia de Concepción.

37. Concepción, vol. 75, March 11, 1824, Archivo Intendencia de Concepción.

38. Nacimiento, March 18, 1824, vol. 75, Archivo Intendencia de Concepción.

39. Concepción, May 31, 1824, vol. 75, Archivo Intendencia de Concepción.

40. Yumbel, May 28, 1824, vol. 75, Archivo Intendencia de Concepción.

41. Yumbel, July 7, 1824, vol. 75, no. 328, Archivo Intendencia de Concepción.

42. Two weeks later Barnachea informs Rivera of an enemy attack on a hacienda named Coyanco in the district of La Laja: "After killing the mayordomo, Anselmo, they fled, taking with them some wine and aguardiente, four horses, four yoke of oxen and two cows." Yumbel, July 26, 1824, vol. 75, no. 343, Archivo Intendencia de Concepción.

43. Pico actively recruited Mariluán's people during his march toward San Carlos in early July 1824. For further details see Yumbel, July 7, 1824, vol. 75, no. 328, Archivo Intendencia de Concepción.

44. Clastres, *Society against the State*, 34–35.

45. Pierre Clastres wrote, "Only one structural, cataclysmic upheaval is capable of transforming primitive society, destroying it in the process: the mutation that causes to rise up within that society, or from outside it, the thing whose very absence defines primitive society, hierarchical authority, the power relation, the subjugation of men, in a word, the State." Clastres, *Society against the State*, 171.

46. Archivo Intendencia de Concepción, Nacimiento, October 22, 1824, vol. 75.

47. Ferrando Keun, *Y Así Nació La Frontera*, 297.

48. Ferrando Keun, 297.

49. Ferrando Keun, 297.

50. August 9, 1820, Archivo Intendencia de Concepción.

51. Yumbel, May 1, 1824, vol. 75, Archivo Intendencia de Concepción.

52. Yumbel, January 27, 1824, vol. 75, no. 162, Archivo Intendencia de Concepción.

53. Yumbel, January 27, 1824, vol. 175, no. 162, Archivo Intendencia de Concepción.

54. Letter from Rafael Burgos to Pedro Barnachea, forwarded to Juan de Dio Rivera, no date, vol. 75, Archivo Intendencia de Concepción.

55. Jones, "Warfare, Reorganization, and Readaptation at the Margins of Spanish Rule," 169.

56. Jones, 176.

57. Jones, 176.
58. Jones, 176.

Chapter Five

1. Téllez L. et al., "El Tratado de Tapihue."
2. Téllez L. et al., 187–90; León, *O'Higgins*, 116–20; Painemal, *Los Tratados*, 293–97. There are three existing versions of this *tratados*, housed in the Biblioteca Nacional and the Biblioteca del Congreso in Chile. The photographed version is the first one listed in this note; the second is a transcribed version at the end of Leon's account of the events in 1817–1818, as is Painemal's version in his thesis. Any translations are mine and are taken from Leon's version.
3. Téllez L. et al., "El Tratado de Tapihue"; Bengoa, *Historia Del Pueblo Mapuche*, 33.
4. Bengoa, *Historia Del Pueblo Mapuche*, 33. The 5.5 million Mapuche casualties were due to disease and war with the Spaniards.
5. Bengoa, 34.
6. León, "Parlamentos y afuerinos," 88.
7. León, 87–119, 93.
8. See chapter 3 for a full discussion of bandits.
9. Boccara, "Políticas indígenas en Chile."
10. Casanueva, "Indios malos en tierras buenas," 68.
11. Casanueva, 56.
12. Casanueva, 113.
13. Méndez, "La organización," 147. Both Spaniards and Mapuches ate wheat, which the Spaniards made sure to supply in copious quantities at parlamentos. Not all Mapuche subgroups ate wheat, however. Pehuenches preferred corn.
14. Méndez, "La organización," 148, 151. For a table on the exorbitant sums spent on wine and other food items, see page 152.
15. Méndez, "La organización," 150.
16. Méndez, 162.
17. Weber, *Bárbaros*.
18. Olivares, "Capítulo XXV," 85.
19. Olivares, 85.
20. Olivares, 84.
21. See León Solis, *Maloqueros y conchavadores*.
22. Lázaro A., "Capítulo IX," 218.
23. Méndez, "La organización," 122.
24. Bengoa, *Historia Del Pueblo Mapuche*, 35; Lázaro A., "Capítulo IX," 216.

25. Real Academia Española, "Diccionario de La Lengua Española—Edición del Tricentenario," *Real Academia Española*, accessed February 2, 2019, http://dle.rae.es/? id=bOcCenM.

26. León, "El Parlamento de Tapihue, 1774," 38–40; Zavala et al., *Los Parlamentos Hispano-Mapuches*.

27. In the seventeenth century, Sebastián de Covarrubias Orozco defined the term *nación* as coming from the Latin *nacio* and meaning "kingdom" or "nation." Sebastián de Covarrubias Orozco, "Biblioteca Virtual Miguel de Cervantes," *Tesoro de La Lengua Castellana o Española*, accessed March 8, 2019, http://www.cervantesvirtual.com/obra-visor/del-origen-y-principio-de-la-lengua-castellana-o-romance-que-oy-se-vsa-en-espana-compuesto-por-el--o/html/00918410-82b2-11df-acc7-002185ce6064_980.html. Other scholars argue that there is a marked difference between a nation as comprised of a set of standard customs, interests, and ideals living under one government or authority, and a nation as a purely political construct, which defines a state. Several scholars argue that a state can exist for a long time without having a nation and that nation-states did not achieve their full potential until the end of the nineteenth and even into the twentieth century. See, for examples, Donoso Rojas, "La idea de nación en 1810," and Konig, "Discursos de identidad."

28. Donoso Rojas, "La idea de nación en 1810," 15.

29. Donoso Rojas, 15.

30. País Mapuche, "Tratado de Tapihue: El reconocimiento de la independencia de la Nación Mapuche," *País Mapuche*, accessed October 25, 2016, http://paismapuche.org/?p=2742. Although this article does not provide an academic viewpoint, it is important nonetheless, since most modern-day Mapuches believe that their ancestors lived in a separate nation-state during the Spanish colonial period. The translation is mine.

31. Zavala et al., *Los Parlamentos Hispano-Mapuches*, 317. The translation is mine.

32. Medina, *Diccionario biográfico colonial de Chile*, 186.

33. Carvallo y Goyeneche, "Colección de historiadores," 372.

34. Carvallo y Goyeneche, 373.

35. Medina, *Diccionario biográfico colonial de Chile*, 186.

36. Quoted in Parentini and Herrera, "Capítulo II," 78.

37. Quoted in Jorge Pinto Rodríguez, "La Araucanía," 46–47.

38. Collier and Sater, *A History of Chile*, 95.

39. Collier and Sater, 95.

40. Collier and Sater, 95.

41. Collier and Sater, 96.

42. Collier and Sater, 96.

43. Casanueva, "Capítulo XII," 306.

44. *Parlamento de Negrete*, 5.

45. *Parlamento de Negrete*, 5. Téllez L. et al., "El Tratado de Tapihue."

46. *Parlamento de Negrete*, 13.

47. *Parlamento de Negrete*, 15.

48. Francisco Inalikang, "Nota al Governador Intendente de la Provincia de Cuyo, José de San Martín, Arroyo de la Laja, octubre 29 de 1814," in Pávez, *Cartas Mapuche*, 130–31.

49. "De la independencia de Chile," *Revista de la Guerra*, n.d., 283. Emphasis is mine.

50. "De la independencia de Chile," 283. Quotation in the original.

51. León, *O'Higgins*, 117; Téllez L. et al., "El Tratado de Tapihue," 187.

52. León; Téllez L. et al., 189.

53. León, 118; Téllez L. et al. Emphasis is mine.

54. León, 117; Téllez L. et al., 187.

55. Tellez et al. make a similar argument in their analysis of the Tapihue Tratado when they argue that the fourteen reducciones have been politically subordinated to a superior power and that the superior power, through an assimilationist lens, dictates the common rules by which these reducciones must function. Téllez L. et al., "El Tratado de Tapihue," 180. Additionally, they argue that it "is in this context that the caciques-governors and their subordinates are nothing more than authorities delegated by the republic. They are *estatizadas* [part of the state]." Téllez L. et al., "El Tratado de Tapihue," 180. The 1826 Tratado de Antuco with the archipelago of Chiloé has similar accords to the 1825 Tapihue Tratado, beginning with the first: "the province and archipelago of Chiloé . . . will be incorporated into the Republic of Chile as an *integral part, and her inhabitants will enjoy in the equality of the same rights as Chilean citizens.*" Vicuña Mackenna and Santos Valenzuela, *Historia Jeneral*, 182–83; Painemal, *Los Tratados*, 298–99. Emphasis is mine.

56. Bengoa, *Historia del pueblo Mapuche*, 197–98.

57. Quoted in Bengoa, 227.

58. Quoted in Bengoa, 231.

59. Letter from Mauricio Barbosa to the minister of war, March 4, 1860, vol. 457, Archivo Ministerio de la Guerra.

60. Letter from Mauricio Barbosa to the minister of war.

61. Letter from Mauricio Barbosa to the minister of war.

62. Letter from Mauricio Barbosa to the minister of war.

63. Téllez L. et al., "El Tratado de Tapihue," 169–90.

64. Tellez et al. make a similar argument. However, they claim that it is because Araucanía is now part of Chilean territory. Having to show identification is just part of the administrative apparatus the Chilean state instituted in the region. See Téllez L. et al., "El Tratado de Tapihue," 181.

65. See chapter 6 for a more comprehensive discussion of citizenship.

66. Domeyko, *Araucanía y sus habitantes*.

Chapter Six

1. Silva Avaria, *Identidad*, 24.
2. Chambers, *Families in War and* Peace, 3.
3. Chambers, 14–15.
4. Wood, *Society of Equality*, 10.
5. Wood, 10.
6. Silva Avaria, *Identidad*.
7. Earle, *Return of the Native*, 163.
8. Crow, *Mapuche in Modern Chile*, 42.
9. Crow, 42.
10. Crow, 43.
11. Woll, *Functional Past*, 19.
12. Casanueva, "Capítulo XII," 297.
13. Casanueva, 297.
14. Woll, *Functional Past*, 77.
15. Donoso, *Vicuña Mackenna*, 235.
16. Vicuña Mackenna and Santos Valenzuela, "La conquista de Arauco," 4, column 2.
17. Vicuña Mackenna and Santos Valenzuela, 4, column 2.
18. Vicuña Mackenna and Santo Valenzuela, 7, column 2.
19. Donoso, *Vicuña Mackenna*, 233.
20. Vicuña Mackenna's *La guerra a muerte* is a military history of the newly created Chilean state's battles against remnants of the Spanish crown in Araucanía from 1819 to 1824, when the few remaining Spanish generals regrouped for another assault on the Chilean creoles. The result was a guerrilla war among Chilean creoles, Spanish officers, Mapuches, and bandits that lasted five bloody years. The outcome was the elimination of the Spanish from this region and a clear path for the Chilean state to outright annex Araucanía and subjugate the Mapuche. The book differs from other works of the period precisely because it pays special attention to the conflicts in Araucanía.
21. Vicuña Mackenna, *La guerra a muerte*, 791.
22. Vicuña Mackenna, 791.
23. Vicuña Mackenna, 791.
24. Burke and Humphrey, *Nineteenth-Century Nation Building*, 102.
25. Bilbao in Casanueva, "Capítulo XII," 302.
26. Casanueva, 302.
27. Bilbao, "Los Araucanos: París, 1847," 194–95.
28. Casanueva, "Capítulo XII," 304.
29. Casanueva, 305.
30. Berkhofer, *White Man's Indian*, 155.
31. Berkhofer, 155.
32. Berkhofer, 155.

33. Sutcliffe, *Sixteen Years in Chile and Peru*, vi–vii. Emphasis is mine.
34. Poeppig, *Un testigo*, 12.
35. Poeppig, 12.
36. Poeppig, 456–57.
37. Poeppig, 398.
38. Poeppig, 407–08.
39. Poeppig, 407–08.
40. Domeyko, *Araucanía y sus habitantes*, 3.
41. Domeyko, 47.
42. Domeyko, 48.
43. Domeyko, 53.
44. Bengoa, *Historia Del Pueblo Mapuche*, 154–55.
45. Bengoa, 161.
46. Quoted in Bengoa, 161.
47. Quoted in Bengoa, 161.
48. Saavedra, *Documentos relativos*, introduction.
49. Quoted in Bengoa, *Historia Del Pueblo Mapuche*, 341.

Chapter Seven

1. Ferrando Keun, *Y Así Nació La Frontera*, 284.
2. Weber, *Bárbaros*, epilogue.
3. Barros Arana, *Historia Jeneral de Chile*, XVI:112n5.
4. Petit, *Los Pincheira*, foreword.
5. Petit, prologue.
6. In his study of Mexico's celebrated bandit Joaquín Murieta, Robert McKee Irwin argues that a cultural "icon may incorporate legend or even myth but is not limited to a single story or cultural meaning. An icon more likely attains its status as such for its elasticity, its attractiveness to multiple peoples, and its ability to signify differently in multiple contexts." McKee, xix.
7. Welcome Chile, "Visit to the Pincheiras Cave."
8. Ferrando Keun, *Y Así Nació La Frontera*, 284.
9. Ercilia y Zúñiga, *La Araucana*.

BIBLIOGRAPHY

Manuscript Sources

Archivo Colección Morla Vicuña
Archivo Intendencia de Chiloé
Archivo Intendencia de Colchagua
Archivo Intendencia de Concepción
Archivo Intendencia de Maule
Archivo Intendencia de O'Higgins
Archivo Intendencia de Talca
Archivo Intendencia de Valparaíso
Archivo Judicial de Cauquenes
Archivo Judicial de Linares
Archivo Judicial de San Felipe
Archivo Vicuña Mackenna
British Foreign Office, General Correspondence, Chile. Indiana University Library, Bloomington

Newspapers

Correo Mercantil, Periódico Comercial, Político y Literario (Santiago)
Diario de Documentos del Gobierno (Santiago)
El Araucano (Santiago)
El Cometa (Santiago)
El Liberal (Santiago)
El Mercurio (Santiago)
El Monitor Imparcial (Santiago)
El Valdiviano Federal (Valdivia)
El Verdadero Liberal (Santiago)
La Bandera Tricolor (Santiago)
La Clave (Santiago)

Revista de la Guerra (Santiago)

Rol del Policía (Santiago)

Digital and Printed Primary Sources

Barros Arana, Diego. *Historia Jeneral de Chile*. 16 vols. Santiago: R. Jover, 1884.

Beauchef, Jorge, and Guillermo Feliú Cruz. *Memorias Militares Para Servir a La Historia de La Independencia de Chile Del Coronel Jorge Beauchef, 1817–1829: Y Epistolario (1815–1840)*. Santiago: Editorial Andrés Bello, 1964.

Bilbao, Francisco. "Los Araucanos: París, 1847." *Revista La Cañada: pensamiento filosófico chileno* 1 (2010).

Bolívar, Simón. *Selected Writings of Bolívar*. New York: Colonial Press, 1951.

Carvallo y Goyeneche. "Colección de historiadores i de documentos relativos a la independencia de Chile: tomo IV." Memoria Chilena, Biblioteca Nacional de Chile. Accessed February 2, 2019. http://www.memoriachilena.cl/602/w3-article-121827.html.

Connelly, Thomas, and Thomas. Higgins. *Diccionario Nuevo de Las Dos Lenguas Espanõla é Inglesa*. Madrid: Imprenta real. por P. J. Pereyra, 1797. https//catalog.hathitrust.org/Record/008619405.

Diccionario Del Poder Mundial. "Estado-Nación." *Diccionario Del Poder Mundial*. Accessed February 2, 2019. http://poder-mundial.net/termino/estado-nacion.

Domeyko, Ignacio. *Araucanía y sus habitantes; recuerdos de un viaje hecho en las provincias meridionales de Chile en los meses de enero y febrero de 1845*. 2nd ed. Biblioteca Francisco de Aguirre 24. Colección Araucanía 1. Buenos Aires: Editorial Francisco de Aguirre, 1971.

Donoso, Ricardo. *Vicuña Mackenna: su vida, sus escritos y su tiempo (1831–1886)*. 2nd ed. Biblioteca Francisco de Aguirre 65. Colección Nación latinoamericana 4. Buenos Aires: Editorial Francisco de Aguirre, 1977.

Encina, Francisco Antonio, and Leopoldo Castedo. *Resumen de la historia de Chile*, vol 2. 8th ed. Santiago: Zig-Zag, 1970.

Ercilia y Zúñiga, Alonso de. *La Araucana*. Córdoba, Argentina: El Cid Editor, 2004. http://ebookcentral.proquest.com/lib/pitt-ebooks/detail.action?docID=3157630.

Errázuriz, Federico. *Chile bajo el imperio de la constitución de 1828*. Santiago: Imprenta Chilena, 1861. https://babel.hathitrust.org/cgi/pt?id=mdp.39015070287043;view=1up;seq=7.

Letelier, Valentín. *Sesiones de Los Cuerpos Lejislativos*. Santiago: Imprenta Cervantes, 1886.

Medina, Jose Toribio. *Diccionario biográfico colonial de Chile*. 2 vols. Santiago de Chile: Imprenta Elzeviriana, 1906.

Memoria Chilena. "Ignacio Domeyko (1802–1889)." Memoria Chilena, Biblioteca Nacional de Chile. Accessed February 2, 2019. http://www.memoriachilena.cl/602/w3-article-646.html.

"Oficio del governador intendente de concepción." *Gobierno Intendente*, December 3, 1825.

Olivares, Miguel de. "Capítulo XXV: Lo restante de esta materia hasta su conclusión." In *Colección de historiadores i de documentos relativos a la independencia de Chile: tomo IV.* Santiago: Imprenta del Ferrocarril, 1861. http://www.memoriachilena. cl/602/w3-article-121827.html.

Orozco, Sebastián de Covarrubias. *Tesoro de La Lengua Castellana o Española.* Biblioteca Virtual Miguel de Cervantes. Accessed October 30, 2018. http://www. cervantesvirtual.com/obra-visor/del-origen-y-principio-de-la-lengua-castellana-o-romance-que-oy-se-vsa-en-espana-compuesto-por-el—o/ html/00918410–82b2–11df-acc7–00218 5ce6064_980. html.

Pérez Rosales, Vicente, Alfonso Calderón, and Enrique Campos Menéndez. *Páginas Escogidas.* Santiago: Editorial Universitaria, 1986.

Pérez Rosales, Vicente, and Rolando Mellafe R. *Ensayo sobre Chile.* Libros de Chile 1. Santiago: Ediciones de la Universidad de Chile, 1986.

Parlamento de Negrete: 27 de febrero de 1803. Santiago: Editorial AYUN, 2008.

Pávez O., Jorge, ed. *Cartas mapuche: siglo XIX.* Colección de documentos para la historia Mapuche. Santiago: CoLibris: Ocho Libros, 2008.

Poeppig, Eduard Friedrich. *Un testigo en la alborada de Chile (1826–1829).* Translated by Carlos Keller R. Colección Historia y documentos. Santiago: Zig-Zag, 1960.

Portales, Diego. *Diego Portales: pintado por si mismo.* Edited by Ernesto de la Cruz and Guillermo Feliú Cruz. Santiago: Ediciones Ercilla, 1941.

Portales, Diego, Ernesto de la Cruz, and Hernán Díaz Arrieta. *Portales íntimo: las mejores cartas del gran ministro.* Santiago: Imprenta Universitaria, 1930.

Portales, Diego José Victor, Ernesto de la Cruz, and Guillermo Feliú Cruz. *Epistolario de Don Diego Portales, 1821–1837; Recopilación y Notas de Ernesto de La Cruz, Con Un Prólogo y Nuevas Cartas, Algunas Recopiladas y Anotadas.* Santiago: Dirección general de prisiones, imp, 1936.

Real Academia Española, "Diccionario de La Lengua Española—Edición del Tricentenario," Real Academia Española. Accessed February 2, 2019. http://dle. rae.es/?id=bOcCenM.

Saavedra, Cornelio. *Documentos relativos a la ocupación de Arauco.* Santiago: Pontificia Universidad Católica, 2009.

Sutcliffe, Thomas. *Sixteen Years in Chile and Peru: From 1822 to 1839.* London: Fisher, Son, and Co., 1841. https://heinonline.org/HOL/Page?handle=hein.cow/spergf 0001&id=1&size=2&collection=cow%20&index=cowbooks.

Vicuña Mackenna, Benjamín, and José Santos Valenzuela. *Historia Jeneral de La República de Chile Desde Su Independencia Hasta Nuestros Días*, vol. 5. Santiago: Imprenta Nacional, 1866.

———. "La conquista de Arauco. Discurso pronunciado en la Cámara de Diputados en su sesión de 10 de agosto por B. Vicuña Mackenna, Diputado por Valdivia." August 1868. Biblioteca del Congreso Nacional. https://www. bcn.cl/estanteriadigital/resultados?terminos=la+conquista+de+arauco.

Zavala, José Manuel, Cristian Lineros Pérez, Gertrudis Payàs, and Laura Hillock

Damm. *Los Parlamentos Hispano-Mapuches, 1593–1803.* Temuco: Universidad
  Católica de Temuco Ediciones, 2015.

Secondary Sources

Adams, Richard E. W., Murdo J. MacLeod, Frank Salomon, Stuart B. Schwartz,
  Bruce G. Trigger, and Wilcomb E. Washburn, eds. *The Cambridge History of the
  Native Peoples of the Americas.* Cambridge: Cambridge University Press, 1996.
Adelman, Jeremy, and Stephen Aron. "From Borderlands to Borders: Empires,
  Nation-States, and the Peoples in between in North American History." *American Historical Review* 104, no. 3 (1999): 814–41. https://doi.org/10.2307/2650990.
Aguirre, Carlos, Charles Walker, and Carmen Vivanco, eds. *Bandoleros, Abigeos y
  Montoneros: Criminalidad y Violencia En El Perú, Siglos XVIII–XX.* Serie
  Tiempo de Historia 7. Lima: Instituto de Apoyo Agrario, 1990.
Alonso, Ana María. *Thread of Blood: Colonialism, Revolution, and Gender on Mexico's
  Northern Frontier.* Tucson: University of Arizona Press, 1995.
Arteaga Alemparte, Justo, and Claudio Orrego Vicuña, eds. *Vicuña Mackenna,
  chileno de siempre.* Santiago: Editorial del Pacífico, 1974.
Axtell, James. *The Invasion Within: The Contest of Cultures in Colonial North America.*
  New York: Oxford University Press, 1985.
Bauer, Arnold J. *Chilean Rural Society from the Spanish Conquest to 1930.* Cambridge
  Latin American Studies 21. Cambridge: Cambridge University Press, 1975.
Bengoa, José. *Historia Del Pueblo Mapuche (Siglo XIX y XX).* Colección Estudios
  Históricos. Santiago: Ediciones Sur, 1985.
Berkhofer, Robert F. *The White Man's Indian: Images of the American Indian from
  Columbus to the Present.* New York: Knopf, 1978.
Bhabha, Homi K., ed. *Nation and Narration.* London: Routledge, 1990.
Bhatia, Michael V. "Fighting Words: Naming Terrorists, Bandits, Rebels and Other
  Violent Actors." *Third World Quarterly* 26, no. 1 (2005): 5–22.
Bieber, Judy. *Power, Patronage, and Political Violence.* Lincoln: University of Nebraska
  Press, 1999.
Birkbeck, Christopher. "Latin American Banditry as Peasant Resistance: A Dead-
  End Trail?" *Latin American Research Review* 26, no. 1 (1991): 156–60.
Blok, Anton. "The Peasant and the Brigand: Social Banditry Reconsidered." *Comparative Studies in Society and History* 14, no. 4 (1972): 494–503.
Boccara, Guillaume, ed. *Colonización, resistencia y mestizaje en las Américas, siglos
  XVI–XX.* Lima: IFEA/Ediciones Abya-Yala, 2002.
———. "Etnogénesis Mapuche: Resistencia y Restructuración Entre Los Indígenas
  Del Centro-Sur de Chile (Siglos XVI–XVIII)." *Hispanic American Historical
  Review* 79, no. 3 (1999): 425–61.
———. "Notas Acerca de Los Dispositivos de Poder En La Sociedad

Colonial-Fronteriza, La Resistencia y La Transculturación de Los Reche-Mapuches Del Centro-Sur de Chile (XVI–XVIII)." *Revista de Indias* 56, no. 208 (December 30, 1996): 659–95.

———. "Políticas indígenas en Chile (siglos xix y xx) de la asimilación al pluralismo-El Caso Mapuche." *Nuevo Mundo Mundos Nuevos*, February 14, 2005, 1–29.

Bolton, Herbert E. "The Epic of Greater America." *American Historical Review* 38, no. 3 (1933): 448–74. https://doi.org/10.2307/1837492.

Bravo, Kléber Antonio. *Bandidos: Una Biografía Indiscreta Del Subdesarrollo Ecuatoriano*. Quito: Abya-Yala, 2001.

Burke, Janet, and Ted Humphrey. *Nineteenth-Century Nation Building and the Latin American Intellectual Tradition*. Indianapolis: Hackett, 2007.

Campos Harriet, Fernando. *Los defensores del rey*. 2nd ed. Santiago: Editorial Andrés Bello, 1976.

Cárcamo-Huechante, Luis E. "Las Trizaduras Del Canto Mapuche: Lenguaje, Territorio y Colonialismo Acústico En La Poesía de Leonel Lienlaf." *Revista de Crítica Literaria Latinoamericana* 40, no. 79 (2014): 227–42.

Casanova Guarda, Holdenis. *Las Rebeliones Araucanas Del Siglo XVIII: Mito y Realidad*. Serie Quinto Centenario 1. Temuco, Chile: Ediciones Universidad de la Frontera, 1987.

Casanueva, Fernando. "Capítulo XII—Indios malos en tierras buenas: visión y concepción del mapuche según las elites chilenas (siglo XIX)." In *Colonización, Resistencia y mestizaje en las américas (siglos XVI–XX)*, edited by Guillaume Boccara, 291–329. Quito: Ediciones Abya-Yala, 2002.

———. "Indios malos en tierras buenas: visión y concepción del mapuche según las elites chilenas del siglo XIX." In *Modernización, Inmigración y Mundo Indígena: Chile y la Araucanía en el siglo XIX*, edited by Jorge Pinto Rodríguez. Temuco, Chile: Universidad de la Frontera, 1998.

Centeno, Miguel Angel. *Blood and Debt: War and the Nation-State in Latin America*. University Park: Pennsylvania State University Press, 2002.

Chambers, Sarah C. *Families in War and Peace: Chile from Colony to Nation*. Durham, NC: Duke University Press Books, 2015. http://site.ebrary.com/lib/alltitles/docDetail.action? docID=11062700.

Clastres, Pierre. *Society against the State: The Leader as Servant and the Humane Uses of Power among the Indians of the Americas*. New York: Urizen Books, 1977.

Colás, Alejandro, and Bryan Mabee, eds. *Mercenaries, Pirates, Bandits and Empires: Private Violence in Historical Context*. New York: Columbia University Press, 2010.

Collier, Simon, and William F. Sater. *A History of Chile, 1808–1994*. Cambridge Latin American Studies 82. Cambridge: Cambridge University Press, 1996.

Contador, Ana María. *Los Pincheira: Un Caso de Bandidaje Social, Chile, 1817–1832*. Santiago: Bravo y Allende Editores, 1998.

Cotelo, Enrique. "Where States Ended and Nations Began: Modernization and

National Identity at the Borderlands of Brazil and Uruguay, 1850–1880." PhD dissertation, University of Mississippi, 2012.

Crow, Joanna. *The Mapuche in Modern Chile: A Cultural History*. Gainesville: University Press of Florida, 2013.

Dabove, Juan Pablo. "Bandidos y Letrados: Violencia Campesina Literatura y Formación de La Nación-Estado En América Latina En El Largo Siglo XIX." PhD dissertation, University of Pittsburgh, 2002.

———. *Bandit Narratives in Latin America: From Villa to Chavez*. Pittsburgh: University of Pittsburgh Press, 2017.

———. *Nightmares of the Lettered City: Banditry and Literature in Latin America, 1816–1929*. Pittsburgh: University of Pittsburgh Press, 2007.

Daitsman, Andy. "Bandolerismo: mito y sociedad, Algunos apuntes teóricos." *Proposiciones* 19 (1990): 263–67.

Dawe, John. "Contesting Cosmologies: Culture and Crime in Nineteenth Century Chile." Paper presented at the conference of the Centro de Estudios y Documentación Latinamericanos, June 6–7, 1996.

De la Fuente, Ariel. *Children of Facundo*. Durham, NC: Duke University Press, 2000.

DeLay, Brian. *War of a Thousand Deserts: Indian Raids and the U.S.–Mexican War*. New Haven: Yale University Press, 2008.

Dillehay, Tom D. *Araucanía, Presente y Pasado*. Santiago: Editorial Andrés Bello, 1990.

———. *Monuments, Empires, and Resistance: The Araucanian Polity and Ritual Narratives*. Cambridge: Cambridge University Press, 2007. http://ebookcentral. proquest.com/lib/pitt-ebooks/detail.action? docID=288641.

———. *The Settlement of the Americas: A New Prehistory*. New York: Basic Books, 2000.

Djenderedjian, Julio. "Roots of Revolution: Frontier Settlement Policy and the Emergence of New Spaces of Power in the Río de La Plata Borderlands, 1777–1810." *Hispanic American Historical Review* 88, no. 4 (2008): 639–68. https://doi. org/10.1215/00182168-2008-003.

Donoso, Ricardo. *Vicuña Mackenna: su vida, sus ecritos y su tiempo (1831–1886)*. 2nd ed. Biblioteca Francisco de Aguirre 65. Colección Nación latinoamericana 4. Buenos Aires: Editorial F. de Aguirre, 1977.

Donoso Rojas, Carlos. "La idea de nación en 1810." *Polis: Revista Latinoamericana*, no. 15 (December 26, 2006). https://polis.revues.org/4999.

Ducey, Michael T. "Village, Nation, and Constitution: Insurgent Politics in Papantla, Veracruz, 1810–1821." *Hispanic American Historical Review* 79, no. 3 (1999): 463–93.

DuVal, Kathleen. *The Native Ground: Indians and Colonists in the Heart of the Continent*. Philadelphia: University of Pennsylvania Press, 2006.

Earle, Rebecca. *The Return of the Native: Indians and Myth-Making in Spanish America, 1810–1930*. Durham, NC: Duke University Press, 2007.

Echeverri, Marcela. *Indian and Slave Royalists in the Age of Revolution: Reform, Revolution, and Royalism in the Northern Andes, 1780–1825*. Cambridge: Cambridge University Press, 2016.

Erbig, Jeffrey Alan Jr.. "Imperial Lines, Indigenous Lands: Transforming Territorialities of the Río de La Plata, 1680–1805." University of North Carolina at Chapel Hill, 2015.

Eyzaguirre, Jaime. *Chile Durante El Gobierno de Errázuriz Echaurren, 1896–1901*. 2nd ed. Santiago: Empresa Editora Zig-Zig, 1957.

Farberman, Judith, Silvia Ratto, and María Mónica Bjerg, eds. *Historias Mestizas En El Tucumán Colonial y Las Pampas (Siglos XVII–XIX)*. Buenos Aires: Editorial Biblos, 2009.

Feliú Cruz, Guillermo, ed. *Cartas Pehuenches; El Telégrafo: 1819–1920*. Colección de Antiguos Periódicos Chilenos 8. Santiago: Imprenta Cultura, 1958.

———. *Conversaciones de Claudio Gay, con algunos de los testigos y actores de la Independencia de Chile, 1808–1826*. Santiago: Editorial Andrés Bello, 1965.

———. "Vicuña Mackenna, El Historiador." In *Vicuña Mackenna: Chileno de Siempre*, edited by Claudio Orrego Vicuña, 160–61. Santiago: Editorial del Pacífico, 1974.

———. *Vicuña Mackenna: Un Historiador Del Siglo XIX: Ensayo*. Santiago: Nascimento, 1950.

Ferrando Keun, Ricardo. *Y Así Nació La Frontera: Conquista, Guerra, Ocupación, Pacificación, 1550–1900*. Biblioteca Francisco de Aguirre 70. Santiago: Editorial Antártica, 1986.

Foerster, Rolf. *Historia de La Evangelización de Los Mapuche*. Santiago: Instituto Nacional de Pastoral Rural, 1992.

———. *Jesuitas y Mapuches, 1593–1767*. Colección Imagen de Chile. Santiago de Chile: Editorial Universitaria, 1996.

Folsom, Raphael Brewster. *The Yaquis and the Empire: Violence, Spanish Imperial Power, and Native Resilience in Colonial Mexico*. New Haven, CT: Yale University Press, 2014. http://site.ebrary.com/lib/alltitles/docDetail.action?docID=10960921.

Frazer, Chris. *Bandit Nation: A History of Outlaws and Cultural Struggle in Mexico, 1810–1920*. Lincoln: University of Nebraska Press, 2006.

Friedman, Jonathan, ed. *Globalization, the State and Violence*. Walnut Creek, CA: AltaMira, 2003.

Góngora, Mario. *Origen de Los "Inquilinos" de Chile Central*. Santiago: Universidad de Chile, Seminario de Historia Colonial, 1960.

Guerra, François-Xavier. *Modernidad e Independencias*, vol. 386. Madrid: Encuentro, 2009.

Guy, Donna J., and Thomas E. Sheridan, eds. *Contested Ground: Comparative Frontiers on the Northern and Southern Edges of the Spanish Empire*. Southwest Center Series. Tucson: University of Arizona Press, 1998.

Haefeli, Evan. "A Note on the Use of North American Borderlands." *American Historical Review* 104, no. 4 (1999): 1222–25. https://doi.org/10.2307/2649570.

Hämäläinen, Pekka. *The Comanche Empire*. Lamar Series in Western History. New Haven, CT: Yale University Press, 2008.

Hennessy, C. A. M. *The Frontier in Latin American History*. London: Edward Arnold, 1978.

Herr, Pilar M. "Indians, Bandits, and the State: Chile's Path toward National Identity (1819–1833)." PhD thesis, Indiana University, 2001. http://search.proquest.com. pitt.idm.oclc.org/pqdtglobal/docview/304698507/abstract/CBE6D2257EA7496 APQ/1.

———. "The Nation-State According to Whom?" *Journal of Early American History* 4, no. 1 (March 14, 2014): 66–94. https://doi.org/10.1163/18770703–00401008.

Hobsbawm, E. J. *Bandits*. Pageant of History Series. New York: Delacorte Press, 1969.

Holdenis, Casanova G. "El rol del jefe en la sociedad Mapuche prehispánica." In *Araucanía: temas de historia fronteriza*, edited by Sergio Villalobos R. and Jorge Pinto Rodríguez. Temuco, Chile: Ediciones Universidad de la Frontera, 1985.

Horsman, Reginald. *Race and Manifest Destiny: The Origins of American Racial Anglo-Saxonism*. Cambridge, MA: Harvard University Press, 1981.

Hoxie, Frederick E. *A Final Promise: The Campaign to Assimilate the Indians, 1880–1920*. Lincoln: University of Nebraska Press, 1984.

Inostrova Córdova, Iván, ed. *Etnografía Mapuche Del Siglo XIX*. Fuentes Para La Historia de La República 13. Santiago: Dirección de Bibliotecas, Archivos y Museos, Centro de Investigaciones Diego Barros Arana, 1998.

Irwin, Robert McKee. *Bandits, Captives, Heroines, and Saints: Cultural Icons of Mexico's Northwest Borderlands*. Cultural Studies of the Americas 20. Minneapolis: University of Minnesota Press, 2007.

Jacoby, Karl. *Shadows at Dawn*. Penguin History of American Life. New York: Penguin, 2008.

Jones, Kristine. "Warfare, Reorganization, and Readaptation at the Margins of Spanish Rule: The Southern Margin (1573–1882)." *Cambridge History of the Native Peoples of the Americas*. Cambridge Core. Accessed February 2, 2019. https://www.cambridge.org/core/books/cambridge-history-of-the-native-peoples-of-the-americas/warfare-reorganization-and-readaptation-at-the-margins-of-spanish-rule-the-southern-margin-15731882/402538A9BDF7997694 1794680D3C02C0.

Jong, Ingrid de. "Armado y Desarmado de Una Confederación: El Liderazgo de Calfucurá En El Período de La Organización Nacional." *Quinto Sol* 13 (January 1, 2009): 11–45.

———. "Funcionarios de Dos Mundos En Un Espacio Liminal: Los 'Indios Amigos' En La Frontera de Buenos Aires (1856–1866)." *Cultura-Hombre-Sociedad* 15, no. 2 (July 1, 2008). https://doi.org/10.7770/cuhso-V15N2-art271.

———. "Historia, Etnicidad y Memoria: El Proceso de Conformación de La Identidad Indígena En La Tribu Amiga de Los Toldos (Provincia de Buenos Aires)." *Corpus* 4, no. 1 (June 30, 2014). https://doi.org/10.4000/corpusarchivos.765.

Joseph, Gilbert M. "On the Trail of Latin American Bandits: A Reexamination of Peasant Resistance." *Latin American Research Review* 25, no. 3 (1990): 7–53.

———. "'Resocializing' Latin American Banditry: A Reply." *Latin American Research Review* 26, no. 1 (1991): 161–74.

Katz, Friedrich, Joint Committee on Latin American Studies, and American Council of Learned Societies, eds. *Riot, Rebellion, and Revolution: Rural Social Conflict in Mexico*. Princeton, NJ: Princeton University Press, 1988.

Konig, Hans-Joachim. "Discursos de identidad, Estado-Nación y ciudadanía en América Latina: Viejos problemas-nuevos enfoques y dimensiones." Paper presented at the Universidad Nacional de Colombia, Medellín, Colombia, March 2003. http://biblioteca.clacso.edu.ar/ar/libros/colombia/fche/histo11.pdf.

Langer, Erick Detlef. "The Eastern Andean Frontier (Bolivia and Argentina) and Latin American Frontiers: Comparative Contexts (19th and 20th Centuries)." *Americas* 59, no. 1 (August 1, 2002): 33–63. https://doi.org/10.1353/tam.2002. 0077.

Langfur, Hal. *The Forbidden Lands*. Stanford, CA: Stanford University Press, 2006.

Lázaro A, Carlos. "Capítulo IX: El parlamentarismo fronterizo en la Araucanía y las Pampas." In *Colonización, resistencia y mestizaje en las Américas (siglos XVI–XX)*, edited by Guillaume Boccara, 201–35. Lima: IFEA/Ediciones Abya-Yala, 2002.

Leiva, Arturo. *El Primer Avance a La Araucanía Angol, 1862*. Temuco, Chile: Ediciones Universidad de la Frontera, 1984.

León, Leonardo. "El Parlamento de Tapihue, 1774" *Nutram* 9, no. 32 (1993).

———. *O'Higgins y la cuestión mapuche: 1817–1818*. Santiago: Ediciones Akhilleus, 2011.

———. *Parlamentos y Afuerinos En La Frontera Mapuche Del Río Bío-Bío (Chile), 1760–1772*. Red Fronteras de la historia, 2009. http: //pitt.idm.oclc.org/login? url=http://site.ebrary.com/lib/pitt/Top? id=10337666.

León Solis, Leonardo, ed. *Araucanía: la frontera mestiza, siglo XIX*. Santiago: LOM Editores, 2003.

———. *La Araucanía: la violencia mestiza y el mito de la "Pacificación," 1880–1900*. Santiago: Universidad ARCIS, Escuela de Historia y Ciencias Sociales, 2005.

———. *Maloqueros y Conchavadores: En Araucanía y Las Pampas, 1700–1800*. Serie Quinto Centenario 7. Temuco, Chile: Ediciones Universidad de la Frontera, 1990.

Lewin, Linda. "The Oligarchical Limitations of Social Banditry in Brazil: The Case of the 'Good' Thief Antônio Silvino." In *Bandidos: The Varieties of Latin American Banditry*, edited by Richard W. Slatta. Contributions in Criminology and Penology 14. New York: Greenwood Press, 1987.

Lihn, Enrique, ed. *Relatos de Bandidos Chilenos*. Santiago: Editorial Sudamericana Chilena, 2001.

Llorens, Miquel Izard. "Ni cuatreros ni montaneros, llaneros." *Boletín americanista* 31 (1981): 83–142.

"Los Pincheira." *Wikipedia, la enciclopedia libre*, January 7, 2017. https://es.wikipedia.org/w/index.php?title=Los_Pincheira&oldid=96075252.

Loveman, Brian. *Chile: The Legacy of Hispanic Capitalism*. 3rd ed. Latin American Histories. New York: Oxford University Press, 2001.

———. *The Constitution of Tyranny: Regimes of Exception in Spanish America*. Pitt Latin American Series. Pittsburgh: University of Pittsburgh Press, 1993.

Méndez, Luz María. "La organización de los parlamentos de indios en el siglo XVIII." In *Relaciones fronterizas en la Araucanía*, edited by Sergio Villalobos R., 109–73. Santiago: Ediciones Universidad Católica de Chile, 1982.

Monsma, Karl. "Fragile Liberty: The Enslavement of Free People in the Borderlands of Brazil and Uruguay, 1846–1866." *Luso-Brazilian Review* 50, no. 1 (2013): 7–25. https://doi.org/10.1353/lbr.2013.0003.

"Nación y Nacionalismo En Chile Resumen." Scribd, April 19, 2016. https://www.scribd.com/document/309756714/Nacion-y-Nacionalismo-en-Chile-Resumen.

Negri, Antonio. "Sobre El Concepto de Estado-Nación." Periódico Diagonal. Accessed February 2, 2019. https://www.diagonalperiodico.net/blogs/fundaciondeloscomunes/sobre-concepto-estado-nacion.html.

Neuman, Henry, and G. Baretti. *Neuman and Baretti's Dictionary of the Spanish and English Languages, Wherein the Words Are Correctly Explained, Agreeably to Their Different Meanings*. Boston: Wilkins, Carter, 1850. https://catalog.hathitrust.org/Record/008678390.

Painemal, Carlos Contreras. *Los Tratados celebrados por los Mapuches con la Corona Española, la República de Chile, y la República de Argentina*. Berlin: Free Universitat Berlin, 2010.

País Mapuche. "Tratado de Tapihue: El reconocimiento de la independencia de la Nación Mapuche." *País Mapuche*, December 28, 2010. http://paismapuche.org/?p=2742.

Parentini, Luis Carlos, and Patricia Herrera. "Capítulo II: Araucanía Maldita: Su Imagen a Través de la Prensa (1820–1860)." In *Araucanía: la frontera mestiza, siglo XIX*, edited by Leonardo León Solis, 63–108. Santiago: LOM Editores, 2003.

Peralta C., Paulina. *¡Chile Tiene Fiesta!: El Origen Del 18 de Septiembre, (1810–1837)*. Historia. Santiago: LOM Ediciones, 2007.

Perez, Louis A. *Lords of the Mountain: Social Banditry and Peasant Protest in Cuba, 1878–1918*. Pitt Latin American Studies. Pittsburgh: University of Pittsburgh Press, 2009. http://digital.library.pitt.edu/cgi-bin/t/text/text-idx?idno=31735057895702;view=toc;c=pittpress.

Petit, Magdalena. *Los Pincheira*. Santiago: Empresa Zig-Zag, 1949.

Pinto Rodríguez, Jorge. "La Araucanía, 1750–1850: Un mundo fronterizo en Chile a fines de la Colonia y comienzos de la República." In *Modernización, inmigración y mundo indígena: Chile y la Araucanía en el siglo XIX*, edited by Jorge Pinto Rodríguez. Temuco, Chile: Ediciones Universidad de la Frontera, 1998.

———, ed. *Misioneros En La Araucanía, 1600–1900: Un Capítulo de Historia Fronteriza En Chile*. Serie Quinto Centenario 2. Temuco, Chile: Ediciones Universidad de la Frontera, 1988.

———, ed. *Modernización, inmigración y mundo indígena: Chile y la Araucanía en el siglo XIX*. Temuco, Chile: Ediciones Universidad de la Frontera, 1998.

Pinto Vallejos, Julio, and Verónica Valdivia Ortiz de Zárate. *Chilenos Todos?: La Construcción Social de La Nación (1810–1840)*. Santiago: LOM, 2009.

Prado, Fabrício. *Edge of Empire: Atlantic Networks and Revolution in Bourbon Rio de la Plata*. Oakland: University of California Press, 2015.

———. "The Fringes of Empires: Recent Scholarship on Colonial Frontiers and Borderlands in Latin America." *History Compass* 10, no. 4 (April 1, 2012): 318. https://doi.org/10.1111/j.1478–0542.2012.00837.x.

Ratto, Silvia. "Estado, Vecinos e Indígenas En La Conformación Del Espacio Fronterizo: Buenos Aires, 1810–1852." *Corpus*, September 16, 2014. https://doi.org/10.4000/corpusarchivos.879.

———. *Indios y Cristianos: Entre La Guerra y La Paz En Las Fronteras*. Nudos de La Historia Argentina. Buenos Aires: Editorial Sudamericana, 2007.

———. "Otras Independencias? Los Territorios Indígenas Rioplatenses En La Década de 1810." *Mundo Agrario* 17, no. 35 (September 1, 2016): e015.

———. *Redes Políticas En La Frontera Bonaerense (1836–1873): Crónica de un Fina Anunciado*, Bernal, Argeninta: Universidad de Quilimes, 2015.

Redclift, M. R. *Frontiers: Histories of Civil Society and Nature*. Cambridge, MA: MIT Press, 2006.

Reséndez, Andrés. *Changing National Identities at the Frontier: Texas and New Mexico, 1800–1850*. Cambridge: Cambridge University Press, 2005.

———. *The Other Slavery: The Uncovered Story of Indian Enslavement in America*. Boston: Houghton Mifflin Harcourt, 2016.

Salazar, Gabriel. *Diego Portales: Monopolista, Sedicioso, Demoledor (Juicio Cuidadano a Un Anti-Demócrata)*. 2nd ed. Santiago: Editorial Universidad de Santiago de Chile, 2014. http://ebookcentral.proquest.com/lib/pitt-ebooks/detail.action?docID=3221294.

Salazar Vergara, Gabriel. *Construcción de Estado En Chile (1760–1860): Democracia de "Los Pueblos," Militarismo Ciudadano, Golpismo Oligárquico*. Santiago: Editorial Sudamericana, 2005.

———. *Labradores, Peones y Proletarios: Formación y Crisis de La Sociedad Popular Chilena Del Siglo XIX*. Santiago: LOM Ediciones, 2000. http://pitt.idm.oclc.org/login?

———. *Mercaderes, Empresarios y Capitalistas: Chile, Siglo XIX*. Santiago: Editorial Sudamericana/Random House Mondadori, 2009.

Salomon, Frank, ed. "The Cambridge History of the Native Peoples of the Americas." Cambridge Core. Accessed February 2, 2019. https://www.cambridge.org/core/books/cambridge-history-of-the-native-peoples-of-the-americas/F0D42D96B3D111DEB3A645F4701DB82F.

Sanders, James E. *The Vanguard of the Atlantic World: Creating Modernity, Nation, and Democracy in Nineteenth-Century Latin America*. Durham, NC: Duke University Press, 2014.

Sarmiento, Domingo Faustino, Mary Tyler Peabody Mann, and Ilan Stavans. *Facundo, or, Civilization and Barbarism*. New York: Penguin, 1998.

Sarmiento, Jacqueline. "Judith Farberman y Silvia Ratto (Coord.) 2009. Historias Mestizas En El Tucumán Colonial y Las Pampas (Siglos XVII–XIX). Buenos Aires: Biblos. 222 P." *Mundo Agrario* 10, no. 20 (July 27, 2010). http://www.mundoagrario.unlp.edu.ar/article/view/v10n20a21.

Shaw, Brent D. "Bandits in the Roman Empire." *Past & Present* 105 (1984): 3–52.

Silva Avaria, Bárbara. *Identidad y nación entre dos siglos: patria vieja, centenario y bicentenario*. Santiago: LOM Ediciones, 2014.

Singelmann, Peter. "Establishing a Trail in the Labyrinth." *Latin American Research Review* 26, no. 1 (1991): 152–55.

Slatta, Richard W., ed. *Bandidos: The Varieties of Latin American Banditry*. Contributions in Criminology and Penology 14. New York: Greenwood Press, 1987.

———. "Bandits and Rural Social History: A Comment on Joseph." *Latin American Research Review* 26, no. 1 (1991): 145–51.

Solares Robles, Ma Laura. *Bandidos Somos y En El Camino Andamos: Bandidaje, Caminos y Administración de Justicia En El Siglo XIX, 1821–1855: El Caso de Michoacán*. Morelia, Mexico: Instituto Michoacano de Cultura: Instituto de Investigaciones Dr. José María Luis Mora, 1999.

Sougarret, Jorge Muñoz. "Milicias Rurales En El Sur Chileno Decimonónico ¿Conflicto Racial O De Poder? El Caso Martín, 1852." *Canadian Journal of Latin American and Caribbean Studies* 32, no. 64 (2007): 155–80.

Taylor, William P. "Banditry and Insurrection: Rural Unrest in Central Jalisco, 1790–1860." In *Riot, Rebellion, and Revolution: Rural Social Conflict in Mexico*, edited by Friedrich Katz, Joint Committee on Latin American Studies, and American Council of Learned Societies. Princeton, NJ: Princeton University Press, 1988.

Téllez L., Eduardo, Osvaldo Silva G., Alain Carrier, and Valeska Rojas C. "El Tratado De Tapihue Entre Ciertos Linajes Mapuches Y El Gobierno De Chile [1825]." *Cuadernos de Historia* 35 (December 2011): 169–90. https://doi.org/10.4067/S0719-12432011000200007.

Thomson, Janice E. *Mercenaries, Pirates, and Sovereigns: State-Building and Extraterritorial Violence in Early Modern Europe*. Princeton Studies in International History and Politics. Princton, NJ: Princeton University Press, 1996.

Turner, Frederick Jackson. *The Early Writings of Frederick Jackson Turner; with a List of All His Works Compiled.* Madison: University of Wisconsin Press, 1938. http://hdl.handle.net/2027/uc1.b3861531.

Turner, Frederick Jackson, and John Mack Faragher. *Rereading Frederick Jackson Turner.* New York: Henry Holt, 1994.

Urbina Carrasco, María Ximena. *Fuentes Para La Historia de La Patagonia Occidental En El Periodo Colonial.* Valparaíso: Ediciones Universitarias de Valparaíso, Pontificia Universidad Católica de Valparaíso, 2014.

———. *La Frontera de Arriba En Chile Colonial: Interacción Hispano-Indígena En El Territorio Entre Valdivia y Chiloé e Imaginario de Sus Bordes Geográficos, 1600–1800.* Valparaíso: Ediciones Universitarias de Valparaíso, Pontificia Universidad Católica de Valparaíso, Centro de Investigaciones Diego Barros Arana, 2009.

Valencia Avaria, Luis. *Anales de La República: Textos Constitucionales de Chile y Registro de Los Ciudadanos Que Han Integrado Los Poderes Ejectivo y Legislativo Desde 1810.* Santiago: Editorial Andrés Bello, 1986.

Valenzuela Márquez, Jaime. *Bandidaje Rural En Chile Central: Curicó, 1850–1900.* Colección Sociedad y Cultura 1. Santiago: Dirección de Bibliotecas, Archivos y Museos, Centro de Investigaciones Diego Barros Arana, 1991.

Vanderwood, Paul J. *Disorder and Progress: Bandits, Police, and Mexican Development.* Rev. ed. Latin American Silhouettes. Wilmington, DE: SR Books, 1992.

———. "Nineteenth-Century Mexico's Profiteering Bandits." In *Bandidos: The Varieties of Latin American Banditry*, edited by Richard W. Slatta. Contributions in Criminology and Penology 14. New York: Greenwood Press, 1987.

Vergara del Solar, Jorge Iván, Hans Gundermann Kröll, and Rolf Foerster. *Estado, Conflicto Étnico y Cultura: Estudios Sobre Pueblos Indígenas En Chile.* Qillqa, Chile: Universidad Católica del Norte: Universidad de Antofagasta, 2013.

Vezub, Julio Esteban. "El Estado Sin Estado Entre Los Araucanos/Mapuches." *Chungará (Arica)* 48, no. 4 (December 2016): 723–27. https://doi.org/10.4067/S0717-35620160004000018.

———. "Llanquitruz y la 'máquina de guerra' mapuche-tehuelche: continuidades y rupturas en la geopolítica indígena patagónica (1850–1880)." *Antíteses*, 2011. http://www.redalyc.org/articulo.oa? id=193321417010.

Vicuña Mackenna, Benjamín. *La guerra a muerte.* 3rd ed. Biblioteca Francisco de Aguirre 44. Buenos Aires: Editorial Francisco de Aguirre, 1972.

Vicuña Urrutia, Manuel. *El París americano: la oligarquía chilena como actor urbano en el siglo XIX.* Santiago: Universidad Finis Terrae, Museo Histórico Nacional, 1996.

Videla Lara, Marisol. "Los parlamentos mapuches de la frontera de Chile (1793–1825)." Repositorio Académico, Universidad de Chile, 2011. http://repositorio.uchile.cl/handle/2250/113750.

Villalobos R., Sergio. *La Vida Fronteriza En Chile.* Madrid: Editorial MAPFRE, 1992.

———. *Los Pehuenches en la vida fronteriza.* Santiago: Ediciones Universidad Católica de Chile, 1989.

———. *Portales, Una Falsificación Histórica*. Colección Imagen de Chile. Santiago: Editorial Universitaria, 1989.

———, ed. *Relaciones fronterizas en la Araucanía*. Santiago: Ediciones Universidad Católica de Chile, 1982.

Villalobos R., Sergio, and Jorge Pinto Rodríguez, eds. *Araucanía: Temas de Historia Fronteriza*. Temuco, Chile: Ediciones Universidad de la Frontera, 1985.

Villar, Daniel, Juan Francisco Jiménez, and Silvia Ratto. *Conflicto, Poder y Justicia En La Frontera Bonaerense, 1818–1832*. Bahí Blanca, Argentina: Departamento de Humanidades, Universidad Nacional del Sur, 2003.

Walker, Charles. "Montoneros, bandoleros, malhechores: criminalidad y política en las primeras décadas republicanas." In *Bandoleros, abigeos y montoneros: criminalidad y violencia en el Perú, siglos XVIII–XX*, edited by Carlos Aguirre, Charles Walker, and Carmen Vivanco. Serie Tiempo de historia 7. Lima: Instituto de Apoyo Agrario, 1990.

Warren, Sarah. "A Nation Divided: Building the Cross-Border Mapuche Nation in Chile and Argentina." *Journal of Latin American Studies*, May 2013.

Weber, David J. *Bárbaros: Spaniards and Their Savages in the Age of Enlightenment*. New Haven, CT: Yale University Press, 2005. http://site.ebrary.com/lib/alltitles/docDetail.action? docID=10176374.

———. *The Spanish Frontier in North America*. New Haven, CT: Yale University Press, 1992.

Welcome Chile. "Visit to the Pincheiras Cave—Chillán." Welcome Chile, 2019. https://www.welcomechile.com/chillan/visit-pincheiras-cave.html.

White, Richard. *The Middle Ground: Indians, Empires, and Republics in the Great Lakes Region, 1650–1815*. Cambridge Studies in North American Indian History. Cambridge: Cambridge University Press, 1991.

Woll, Allen. *A Functional Past: The Uses of History in Nineteenth-Century Chile*. Baton Rouge: Louisiana State University Press, 1982.

Wood, James. *Society of Equality: Popular Republicanism and Democracy in Santiago de Chile, 1818–1851*. Albuquerque: University of New Mexico Press, 2011.

Wunder, John R., and Pekka Hämäläinen. "Of Lethal Places and Lethal Essays." *American Historical Review* 104, no. 4 (1999): 1229–34. https://doi.org/10.2307/2649572.

Younger, Joseph P. "'Monstrous and Illegal Proceedings:' Law, Sovereignty and Revolution in the Río de La Plata Borderlands, 1810–1880." PhD dissertation, Princeton University, 2011.

———. "'Naturals of This Republic:' Slave Law, Sovereignty, and the Legal Politics of Citizenship in the Rio de La Plata Borderlands, 1845–1864." *Law and History Review* 30, no. 4 (November 1, 2012): 1099. https://doi.org/10.1017/S0738248012000521.

Zavala, José Manuel. *Los mapuches del siglo XVIII: dinámica interétnica y estrategias de resistencia*. Santiago: Editorial Universidad Bolivariana, 2008.

INDEX

Page numbers in italic text indicate illustrations.

R — 9 — $\overline{VI}$ — 20
T   14 — $\overline{VI}$ — 20